PRAISE FOR
NEUROMINED

"As a polymath, Robert Grant is particularly well suited to diagnose the dystopian cultural dilemma with maximum breadth and precision. This book is a devastating blow to the tyranny of our tech-fueled corporatocracy."

–AUBREY MARCUS, podcaster, *New York Times*
best-selling author, and entrepreneur

"*Neuromined* is a *must-read*! This book will inspire the masses to wake up and regain their technological sovereignty. We need leaders in this field like Robert Grant and Michael Ashley to help guide humanity in the right direction."

–BILLY CARSON, entrepreneur and
founder of 4BiddenKnowledge TV

"Our freedoms are at risk, and everyone is being put in a technical prison by Big Tech, but they are so clever that no one is aware of what is happening. The scariest part is that by the time everyone becomes aware, it will be too late. Fortunately, there are true freedom fighters like Robert and Michael who are raising the curtain to make everyone aware of what is happening. This book is a must-read for anyone with a computer or a smartphone. What makes me so excited about this amazing book is that it not only points out the problem but gives a clear and effective solution that anyone can apply immediately."

–DR. ERIC COLE, CEO and founder of Secure Anchor

"Surveillance capitalism doesn't have to be our reality. Power belongs in the hands of the individual. If you want to understand our technological threat—and how to overcome it—read *Neuromined*."

–LISA WOOD, CEO of Analog Computation
Enterprise and Cognitive World

"Technology is a two-edged sword; it may be used for both good and evil. Authors Grant and Ashley brilliantly show us how to go in the right direction with our shared technological future. This is a must-read book for both techies and non-techies."

–MARK VICTOR HANSEN, best-selling author and
cocreator of the Chicken Soup for the Soul series

"*Neuromined* could easily overwhelm readers with a barrage of complex ideas, harming the public's ability to make sense of our pressing challenge. Instead, Robert and Michael found ingenious ways to connect audiences with the material, both rationally and emotionally. Anyone who encounters this book is bound to be blown away by its power to grip the imagination while also delivering facts essential to understanding our collective challenge—and opportunity. Both a stunning wake-up call and a rallying cry for needed change, this book is essential reading for everyone, no matter their nationality or politics."

—**HER MAJESTY DIAMBI KABATUSUILA,** Queen of the Bakwa
Luntu People of the Democratic Republic of Congo

"In a world in which technology has threatened to take over free will, *Neuromined* leans into this scary prospect and presents a logical plan to maintain our independence. Michael Ashley and Edward Grant offer a first-class case for preventing the final takeover of the human mind by a centralized authority and Big Tech. Unlike with most discussions surrounding this topic, however, it's clear reading this book that there is a way to win the war and an opportunity to leverage technology for our individual benefit, as the Founding Fathers would have wanted."

—**ANDREW GRUEL,** founder of Slapfish and CEO of
American Gravy Restaurant Group

"*Neuromined* offers a brilliant perspective of a beautiful world ahead for many generations to enjoy and thrive in, while highlighting certain threats for our society to avoid by taking clever actions now."

—**TOUFI SALIBA,** author of TODA/IP and global chair of
the IEEE International Protocols for AI Security

"*Neuromined* touches on the most important topic of our time: digital technologies have enslaved users to serve corporate objectives over their own self-interests and, in the process, eradicated the ability of millions of people to apply critical thinking skills against the weaponization of tech, to the detriment of public discourse on a global level."

—**CHRISTIAN KAMEIR,** managing partner at Sustany Capital and
chair of the Decentralized Identity Foundation's
Banking and Finance initiative

"Robert Grant and Michael Ashley deliver a poignant wake-up call in this exposé of the technocracy threatening to undermine the foundation of this country laid out by our Founding Fathers. It's also a powerful call to action for loyal patriots and concerned citizens, leaving readers with this critical question: Are we too late?"

—**HAL WALBRINK,** medical device entrepreneur
and founder and CEO of Xinetix

"While we have acted as dutiful consumers (under the threat of cancelation), parroting the virtues of connectedness and the internet's utopian promises, a nightmarish dystopia has descended, replete with government utilization of the surveillance economy to yield a surveillance politic, eviscerating basic rights in the name of 'progress' or 'safety.' The private citizen is dead. In its place stands a hollowed-out humanity, a predictable consumer unit, utterly dependent, totally subject, and always exposed. Until now. Grant and Ashley boldly lobby for an alternative way to live as authentic human beings by disowning dystopia and recapturing deeply human elements of personal presence. Power down, unplug, and listen to their clarion call to reject our digital wasteland."

–**REVEREND JOHN J. BOMBARO,** PhD, U.S. Navy Reserve
commander and assistant director of theological education
at the Luther Academy, Riga, Latvia

"Robert and Michael expose the core challenge of our times in a straightforward and easily understood manner, invoking pop cultural references and historical examples. Insightful and entertaining, *Neuromined* presents sound arguments against technocratic control based on considerable research and expertise on this subject. I would recommend this book to anyone who wants to know what's really happening in the world today and the many dangers to come should we not respond to our shared threats."

–**GEORGE R. WENTZ,** managing partner at MAD Energy

"From the very first chapter, *Neuromined* pulls you in like a thousand 'likes' on your latest Insta post. Today's tech is both indispensable and inescapable. Most of us can't imagine a day without our iPhone. Or how such addictive devices are already manipulating us.

Grant and Ashley's vision for our future—should we not heed their warning—is reminiscent of Benjamin Franklin's 225-year-old quote: 'Those who would give up essential liberty to purchase a little temporary safety deserve neither liberty nor safety.' The liberty we are clicking away to mega-tech is more than just a little scary. It is downright *WTF are we thinking?*

The relinquishment of liberty Franklin warns against may be found in the fine print of Facebook's and other social media's user agreements. Akin to the metaphoric frog-in-the-boiling-water syndrome, it's enabling big government and Big Tech to freely discriminate against those who do not fall in lockstep with the 'new normal.' To avoid such a fate, tell everyone you know to read this book."

–**PAUL J. NELSON,** founding and managing partner at
Nelson Kirkman Family Law Attorneys and Advisors

"I have said for years that a book needs written about the evolution of our society and how it has been drastically altered by the smartphone and the related technologies it fostered. It has become a calculated intrusion into every aspect of life. Digital domains fashion our beliefs, behaviors, and outcomes. Technology is facilitating the most successful power play in history. We've not only willfully embraced it but celebrated its every intrusion as a necessity. Can our world sustain this? Finally, a well-written book characterizing this era correctly and daring the reader to recognize the risks and crisis we face in this technological tyranny."

—**SCOTT BLEDSOE,** high-tech CEO, composer, and land steward

"More than any other book in recent memory, *Neuromined* makes the persuasive case for decentralizing technology to solve our many crises. If you weren't already convinced that blockchain, crypto, and other decentralized innovations hold the promise to combat Big Tech and big government collusion, you will be by the time you're done reading it. Knowledgeable thought leaders with a passion for this subject, Grant and Ashley demonstrate the importance of data sovereignty in the age of surveillance capitalism, digital cancel culture, shadow banning, and financial deplatforming. If you want to talk intelligently about what's really going on in the zeitgeist, you'd better get familiar with this eye-opening material."

—**DUSTIN PLANTHOLT,** founder of MonteCrypto and Crypterns and editor for Forbes Monaco

"I have been a fan of Michael Ashley's books for the last five years, but especially now, after reading *Neuromined*. I believe Michael and coauthor Robert Edward Grant have given us a book that so many Americans will read and say, 'This is exactly how I feel about the current situation between the government, the corporate world, and everyone else caught up in this almost unimaginable crisis.' I truly hope this effort by Ashley and Grant gets the response it deserves. More than any other book out there, it provides the reader with an insider's view of what's happening every day in the tech world, why they should care, and more importantly, how we fix it."

—**JAMES G. JALET III,** president and CEO of JNR Incorporated

"Grippingly entertaining, yet terrifying at the same time. Grant and Ashley raise the core issues of our day. Spoiler alert: They are not the cultural wedge issues the media insists we focus on. Instead, the two authors tap into the perils of technocracy, which threatens to destroy our way of life—and our children's. Written in a unique, novelistic style and packed with facts, *Neuromined* fearlessly exposes centralized abuses of power that are not in some far-reaching future dystopia but instead are right around the corner."

—**KURT BUSCH,** CEO of Syntiant

NEURO**MINED**

NEURO**MINED**

TRIUMPHING OVER TECHNOLOGICAL TYRANNY

ROBERT EDWARD GRANT

MICHAEL ASHLEY

FAST
COMPANY
Press

Fast Company Press
New York, New York
www.fastcompanypress.com

This work is being published under the Fast Company Press imprint by an exclusive arrangement with *Fast Company*. *Fast Company* and the *Fast Company* logo are registered trademarks of Mansueto Ventures, LLC. The Fast Company Press logo is a wholly owned trademark of Mansueto Ventures, LLC.

Distributed by Greenleaf Book Group

For ordering information or special discounts for bulk purchases, please contact Greenleaf Book Group at PO Box 91869, Austin, TX 78709, 512.891.6100.

Design and composition by Greenleaf Book Group
Cover design by Greenleaf Book Group and Will Weyer

Grateful acknowledgment is made to the following sources for permission to reproduce copyrighted material:

David Higham Associates Ltd.: From "Do Not Go Gentle into That Good Night," in *The Collected Poems of Dylan Thomas* by Dylan Thomas. Copyright © 1952 by the Dylan Thomas Trust. Reproduced by permission.

New Directions Publishing Corp.: From "Do Not Go Gentle into That Good Night," in *The Poems of Dylan Thomas* by Dylan Thomas. Copyright © 1952 by Dylan Thomas. Reproduced by permission.

Publisher's Cataloging-in-Publication data is available.

Print ISBN: 978-1-63908-034-2

eBook ISBN: 978-1-63908-036-6

Audiobook ISBN: 978-1-63908-035-9

To offset the number of trees consumed in the printing of our books, Greenleaf donates a portion of the proceeds from each printing to the Arbor Day Foundation. Greenleaf Book Group has replaced over 50,000 trees since 2007.

Printed in the United States of America on acid-free paper

23 24 25 26 27 28 29 30   10 9 8 7 6 5 4 3 2 1

First Edition

For my children (and future grandchildren),
who deserve to live and prosper in a thriving and free society

—Robert

For Teddy and Sammy—
and all the future Teddys and Sammys

—Michael

CONTENTS

Foreword by Brittany Kaiser   xv

Introduction   1

PART I: Problem   7

   1: The Smartphone Shackle   9

   2: ~~Ministry~~ Monopoly of Truth   25

   3: The Company Line   43

   4: Pan0pticon   61

   5: iNsights   75

   6: Dreams Become Nightmares   95

PART II: Solutions   111

   7: Running Dark   113

   8: #Iniquitous   131

   9: Whac-A-Mole   147

10: You Will Own Nothing and Be Happy   167

Notes   187

About the Authors   197

FOREWORD

Quantum computing puts everyone's data security in jeopardy, and it could ultimately make privacy obsolete. I have seen this statement, and many similar ones, on slides at top technology conferences around the globe. A world without privacy? Well, as a Big Tech whistleblower, I know that we already live in a world where our data is owned by everyone except us, but I didn't always see the tech industry as so foreboding. In fact, I have always believed, and continue to believe, that technology is here to improve our lives, but now I know that we must be careful about who is steering our fate and take data security into our own hands.

My life in technology began the way it does for most young people: excitement about a big career opportunity that was going to include a lot of on-the-job learning with new tech tools. I certainly wasn't an expert yet; I was a bright-eyed and idealistic nineteen-year-old who had managed to be awarded a position with Senator Barack Obama's first presidential campaign using the digital skills I had gained in my personal life and while pursuing passion projects. This new gig as the senator's intern was going to teach me what I needed to know to eventually be eligible for a paid job in the industry, and I was ready to absorb all the exciting projects going on at campaign headquarters. Little did I know that I'd end up creating Barack Obama's first Facebook page, making decisions about how to address online harassment and cyberbullying, helping build the first data-driven political tools on social media, and contributing to the most successful digital campaign of the time.

I started to see that using data-driven tools was like wielding an invisible magic wand: we would release segmented communications, tailored for certain groups and targeted at certain citizens because of the behavioral data that we had analyzed, and then we would see vast spikes in engagement, sign-ups, voter registrations, donations, and more. Our success grew, as did the data products we built, and our campaign became a digital firm, eventually even spinning out a new data science company after the successful election in November 2008. On that election night—which happened to fall on my my twenty-first birthday—I was in awe of what data science could do for politics, humanity, and the world.

So, instead of joining most of the Obama for America campaign team for administration jobs in the White House, I decided to continue with my human rights law studies and travel the world working for human rights nonprofits, teaching them about the fantastic world of data-driven strategies. The deeper I dove into the tech world, the more I felt like I was finding the holy grail and unlocking secrets to accomplishing anything I set my mind to. I saw that the digital strategies I had learned could help solve the world's biggest problems, from stopping hunger to predicting and preventing war. I delved into these topics both academically and practically, theorizing in the academic world and then testing my hypotheses in the field with huge successes.

Many years later in that journey, I would enter Cambridge Analytica, the data science company that used Facebook data in elections, with a similar naive optimism, believing that technology, and specifically data science, could change the world for the better and allow all the incredible organizations that I cared so deeply about to be successful in their campaigns, in their fundraising, in their legislative goals—in anything at all that they wanted to achieve. What I hadn't considered, unfortunately, is that not everyone wields power for good. And that unbridled data collection, paired with an irresponsible application of the technology, could lead to deep and pervasive consequences that were nearly impossible to predict or control.

Through my four years at Cambridge Analytica, across the more than fifty countries I designed data science projects in, I learned that every single person has a digital footprint—an invisible collection of all the personal information that gets siphoned from our daily activities. This nearly incalculable data profile is collected, bought, and sold around the globe, ending up in millions of databases, where it is held and used by anyone and everyone for any purposes, without the explicit consent of the individuals whose data is being employed. The now (in)famous example of Cambridge Analytica and Facebook using our data to intervene in and influence elections is *still* being replicated daily. With the right amount of money, you can buy and use people's data to influence their behavior.

Both governmental and nongovernmental organizations can use the data collected by companies to track private citizens. The extent of this surveillance was most notably revealed in 2013 by National Security Agency whistleblower Edward Snowden, who told the world about the use of data in the PRISM project to track people globally. Data collection took an even darker turn during the COVID-19 shutdown, when Big Tech companies were issued government contracts for contact tracing, direct-location surveillance to map who has come into contact with whom. This was originally announced as a public health program to help save lives and stop the spread of the virus, but it was later found to have been abused by law enforcement and government agencies to spy on citizens for other purposes, like arresting peaceful protesters amid the rise of the Black Lives Matter movement.

Of course, it's not just governments that commit these kinds of data and human rights abuses. Through my work at Cambridge Analytica, designing data programs on nearly every continent, I learned that our data profiles are a major source of power and value for the company that employs them—for its own purposes. Our personal information is a multitrillion-dollar-a-year industry, yet none of this value is coming back to us, the producers of these data sets. Instead, data is usually owned by the company that collects it, not by the citizens producing it. I learned that in most countries, we have few, if any, rights to our data, even though we produce it. I learned that almost no schools or parents practice digital literacy education before giving children unfettered access to devices. I also learned that most databases are easily hackable, lacking proper cybersecurity standards or encryption protocols, and therefore the big data industry is rife with abuse and has an extensive black market. From targeted disinformation to paid influence campaigns, cyberbullying, voter suppression, hacking, phishing, and more, irresponsibly built technology infrastructure was everywhere I looked, and there was (and is) a lot to be done to clean up the mess.

After seeing the darkest side of technology and the data industry, I became a whistleblower, bent on creating a wave of change across the legislative, educational, and technological arenas implicated in my revelations. I showed politicians, executives, and the public alike my evidence of how easily these technologies can be abused and the danger this poses to democracy and human rights. I launched the Own Your Data campaign to explain that I was here not just to highlight the dangers of uncontrolled data collection but also to present solutions: what data ownership, control, and permission structures can achieve when implemented on a large scale. I have worked tirelessly on legislative drafting and passing of new laws regarding data protection, and I have traveled globally to do lectures, run workshops, and scale access to digital literacy. What I have learned through whistleblowing and the Own Your Data campaign is that nothing will protect people as quickly as upgrading the technologies we use in our daily lives.

On this journey, I was blessed to work with some of the world's best documentary filmmakers, who followed me in my work, eventually featuring me in *The Great Hack*, a film released on Netflix in 2019. Hundreds of millions of people around the world saw for the first time a vivid illustration of the problems with the big data industry, the human rights implications, and the vast legal and ethical quandaries we all have to grapple with to find a more equitable way forward for tech and humanity. As *The Great Hack* became Netflix's most popular content worldwide, we were short-listed for an Oscar and nominated for a BAFTA and an Emmy, and the campaign to raise awareness at the global level grew louder and stronger. On a daily basis, I am still recognized wherever I go and thanked for the courage it takes to work for change against such a powerful industry.

But, you may ask, is Big Tech really *that* powerful? In 2017, the *Economist* proclaimed that our digital assets had become the most valuable asset on the planet, surpassing oil and gas.[1] The world's most valuable companies, worth hundreds of billions or even trillions of dollars, were tech companies whose valuations were based on the amount of personal data they had collected from unsuspecting users. Every move that each of us has made—every credit card swipe, every online search, every like or share—has fueled the world's most profitable industry, informing advertising, communications, and strategic decision making by most private and public organizations. Our global, interconnected world has morphed into a state of what Shoshana Zuboff calls *surveillance capitalism*, in which we are the product being sold by most of the companies whose platforms we use every day.[2] Instead of companies sharing the vast value created by every user's data with the people who produced it, they have become extractive, pulling as much data from unsuspecting users as possible and using it to bolster their own valuations, profits, and power.

Now, why is this so dangerous? you may wonder. It seems simple and straightforward: of course we would all like to see only advertisements for things we are likely to want to buy and content that we are likely to want to read or engage with. But over the years, the algorithms that continually target us with this tailored content have invaded privacy, suppressed votes, inflamed conflicts into mass violence, and degraded our civil society significantly. Our very newsfeeds are controlled by centralized decision makers who design the algorithms that govern our entire digital lives, affecting our perspectives and worldviews, all while producing a population whose free speech is strangled, making independent decisions nearly impossible.

This dark influence that the big data behemoths wield is so powerful that our sense of self, as well as public order at large, is in question. Can we really have free and fair elections? Can we really control our daily lives, protect our children, or empower free thought? *Neuromined* dives deep into these fissions within our society. Robert Grant and Michael Ashley take an accessible, story-driven approach to both the dangers of centralized control abetted by technology and the opportunities that exist in the big data crisis, showing how we can all play a role in rebuilding our society to be better, stronger, and more protected than ever before. *Neuromined* presents these problems in an exquisite show-and-tell format, illustrating the harms through stories that everyday people can viscerally connect with and explaining the real-world context to provide proof for the arguments grounded in the stories. It's a balance of art and science that only a brilliant mind like Robert's could achieve.

I first was introduced to Robert not long after I became a

whistleblower and launched the Own Your Data campaign in mid-2018. He told me of his dreams of solving the data-ownership problem and showed me some incredible mathematical work he had done and some new discoveries he had made that would allow quantum-resistant encryption to be possible. He was building a company to research and develop his theorems and create tools that people could use to protect their personal data and empower themselves. I was inspired to find a kindred spirit and joined his advisory team in the early days of Crown Sterling.

Since then, the team's phenomenal developments have made me confident that it's possible to solve the problems of Big Tech and create sustainable and ethical products that people can trust in the long term. Working alongside many of the brightest minds in cryptography, data ethics, and blockchain technology, I believe we are at the precipice of something remarkable. It is an honor to serve on the advisory board, ensuring integrity of decision making, ethics, and data protection practices. I feel that the team has contributed, and will continue to contribute, to the longevity of the data-ownership school of thought, and I am excited to see the road to true data protection unfolding from here.

Before you embark on this journey with Robert and Michael and their seminal work, I want you to remember why I am here and why so many of us have come here: it is because, when employed properly and built to last, technology will make our lives better. Like the late, great Dr. Stephen Hawking said, "Everyone can enjoy a life of luxurious leisure if the machine-produced wealth is shared,"[3] by which he meant that we build products to make sure we can pursue our passions and live full lives, while technology ensures that we can financially secure our basic human rights and more. It is with this passion and intention that I thank you for picking up this book, and I look forward to having you join our rising swell of data-ownership activists, working for a better world and a more secure future.

Brittany Kaiser
Cofounder of the Own Your Data Foundation and author of *Targeted: The Cambridge Analytica Whistleblower's Inside Story of How Big Data, Trump, and Facebook Broke Democracy and How It Can Happen Again*

INTRODUCTION

We hold these truths to be self-evident, that all men are created equal, that they are endowed by their creator with certain unalienable rights, that among these are life, liberty, and the pursuit of happiness. That to secure these rights, governments are instituted among men, deriving their just powers from the consent of the governed. That whenever any form of government becomes destructive of these ends, it is the right of the people to alter or to abolish it, and to institute new government, laying its foundation on such principles, and organizing its powers in such form, as to them shall seem most likely to effect their safety and happiness.

–The Declaration of Independence,
July 4, 1776

FROM SOVEREIGN TO SOVEREIGN GOVERNMENT

We have long been students of the Declaration of Independence. According to this priceless document, the reason for government is to "ensure certain unalienable rights," including "life, liberty, and the pursuit of happiness."

The Founding Fathers wished to create a new governance model. In their vision, government was not simply entitled to power over us. It was meant to serve individuals who have consented to a mutually beneficial relationship. This was a big shift from the preceding millennia. Until this time, a central authority wielded control over the masses.

The 1776 American Revolution sparked similar political uprisings, leading to widespread democracies the world over. As with most social transformations, economics and the desire for sovereignty drove the change.

Finally, in 1789, our Founding Fathers codified the themes of individual rights and freedoms into what we now know as the Bill of Rights. Importantly, they enshrined free speech as the First Amendment:

> Congress shall make no law respecting an establishment of religion, or prohibiting the free exercise thereof; or abridging the freedom of speech, or of the press; or the right of the people peaceably to assemble, and to petition the Government for a redress of grievances.

Free speech is critical to the greatness of the American experience. It allows for dissent. It protects the right to practice religion as we see fit. It also safeguards appropriate public demonstration. Yet these days, all our rights are under fire—especially our ability to speak our minds.

Big Tech, working with our now *Big Government*, silences those who dare speak up. They stop us from sharing links to articles or videos. More secretly, they "shadow ban" content, so users don't even know they are being blocked.

Meanwhile, cancel culture has infected our social discourse. Say the wrong thing, and you can expect to be deplatformed. We can lose our job or our reputation. This leads to a chilling effect, whereby people self-censor.

This wasn't what our founders wished. It wasn't supposed to be this way.

FROM SOVEREIGN GOVERNMENT TO SOVEREIGN CORPORATION

In 2018, data surpassed oil as the world's most valuable asset. Today, surveillance capitalists, using technological capabilities our founders could scarcely imagine, exploit us using our data. Big Tech corporations monetize it to predict and modulate our collective and individual consciousnesses.

This data fuels an attention economy, affecting nations, families, and individuals. Social media, its lifeblood, profits from outrage and anger. Fostering societal polarity and extreme views, it produces weakened empathy for others, especially those holding countervailing opinions. Even our sense of history is under fire by a dubious marriage of government and big business, ripping apart the fabric of what America and being American means.

Nowadays, the illusion of choice is maintained for "the public good," to manufacture public consent. Unfortunately, this illusion frequently runs up against barriers in real life. For instance, contradicting so many illusions of personal agency, free thought is often termed "unacceptable" by an ever-expanding government narrative, political bias, and mass manipulation via the latest weapon of twenty-first-century propaganda: selective (digital) exposure.

Now that our digital personas have fast become a big part of how we assimilate into society, something momentous and nefarious is underway. A war for our minds rages daily online, enabled by the same tech platforms that were supposed to improve life for all.

Instead of being the free people our founders once imagined, in the twenty-first century, the real victors of the American experience appear not to be persons at all. Instead, corporations and government now wield unbelievable power.

FROM SOVEREIGN CORPORATION TO SOVEREIGN INDIVIDUAL

Anyone who has ever played Monopoly can appreciate the dangers of such unfettered control. Once a rival amasses all the properties of a single color, they can charge much higher rent to players, making it harder to travel unscathed. The problem intensifies as an opponent adds houses and then hotels. Before long, anyone who lands on those squares can expect to lose a lot of money—and if it's a wealthy neighborhood, their shirt, too.

Unchecked, centralized technological control can exert the same stranglehold—but in real life. Here's an example. Once upon a time, Main Street USA sold their wares directly to the public. They enjoyed the commerce of passing foot traffic. Not so much these days. Many of today's small businesses must fight for market share on Amazon, one central site. Now, what happens if Amazon decides to delist a store one day? Poof. It's gone.

This same power is also applied to free speech when only a handful of technopolies own and control how we access information.

Despite these threats, we needn't fear for the future. As essayist Ralph Waldo Emerson once said, "This time, like all times, is a very good one, if we but know what to do with it."[1]

A host of decentralizing innovations, like blockchain, cryptocurrencies, non-fungible tokens, smart contracts, peer-to-peer payments/lending, crowdsourcing, and digital distributed ledgers can undermine the threat of monopolistic control over our lives. Likewise, a new data bill of rights we put forward in the pages to come can (finally) make our data our own property.

Undoubtedly, in every black cloud exists a silver lining. This is the case in our current time. In addition to the above, after thousands of years of *human doing*, today, *human beings* can at last create value just through our behaviors, without the need for excessive sweat and toil. This means that the simple act of existing, and thereby producing data every day, can actually be profitable—not just for Big Tech companies but also for us, the people, who rightfully should own our data.

From our vantage point, we see a better future for our world:

one based on the foundation of individual data and real sovereignty; greater personal responsibility; more efficient democracy, allowing for greater freedoms; and importantly, a new potential to *thrive* and not just *survive* as humans.

Such a breakthrough can't come quickly enough.

Much of the liberty we now take for granted came from Johannes Gutenberg's revolutionary acceleration of informational flow hundreds of years ago, when he built the first mechanized printing press. An informed public is one capable of advocating for itself. Embracing this viewpoint, *Neuromined* brings awareness to our crisis and shows the way out.

Meant to reach both hearts and minds, each of the following chapters offers what we call a *show-and-tell* approach. The *show* section presents a short fictional story to emotionally connect you with a real-world topic threatened by unprecedented technological control, including mental health, history, business, social media, education, civil rights, travel, the arts, news media, and activism.

The *tell* portion presents the real-world context for the problem, a related argument, and ways we might correct the situation. Our ambition is to wake people up to centralized tyranny and to ignite an emergent movement toward liberty-minded tech. Aligned in common purpose and deepmost desire, together, we can reclaim our liberty, humanity's birthright—the sweetest treasure we have ever known.

PART I

PROBLEM

1

THE SMARTPHONE SHACKLE

SHOW

The buzz from the phone startles me awake. Sliding my finger across the touch screen, I turn off my alarm. Ben slept next to me after all. Airbuds in. He must have fallen asleep to YouTube again. Or watching Prime.

I must get up soon. Gotta feed Kylie. But there's a little time now. *Time just for me.* Besides, last night was bad. A little me-time will take my mind off the purplish splotch on the wall. The broken glass. And all that came before it.

Opening Facebook on my phone, I'm greeted with notifications.

"OurFamily" is the name of our private FB group. I go to it first. Kelsey, my sis-in-law, posted pics of a day at the beach with her boys. I swipe through each, liking some, loving others. Leaving little hearts.

"Luv you guys," I write. "Miss that Newport sun."

Ben sighs and turns in bed.

Please don't wake yet. I'm not ready to deal with you.

Then I'm on to my feed.

Scrolling down, I see right away that my best friend, Skylar, got that new job she wanted so bad. Matching ring lights perch atop her screens like dual hood ornaments. Behind her, she's set up green plants between her mounted diplomas. I can already picture her Zooming with dignitaries in far-flung countries.

"First day with my new team. It's like I'm in Singapore, right?" Below her post is a winking emoji.

A dog-eared *Fodor's* travel guide appears in my mind's eye. Nearly thirty years later, I can still picture it beside our two rucksacks in some dodgy Amsterdam hostel. More memories fill my mind: long legs flopping down from the bunk bed above me; these belong to a younger Skylar. As I remember those halcyon days, a pain like homesickness fills me. I sigh, wondering where the years went.

"Lucky!" I type to Skylar, wondering how our parents ever let us backpack through Europe without even so much as an email. I don't let Kylie go to school without bringing her phone. And that's five minutes from our house.

There's more news about the Taiwan situation on my newsfeed, but it's too depressing, so I sneak out of bed, one leg at a time, so I won't disturb Ben. Snatching my own Airbuds off the nightstand, I patter over to the bathroom. A MyHome bio-alert tells me that Kylie is already up and in the bathroom.

"Morning, Sunshine," I textalk her. In my head I picture the walls going pink as an AI simulacrum of my voice intones the message.

"What was *that* about last night?" she textalks me back, making my own bathroom flicker a green shade as her words vibrate back in my Airbuds.

"Nothing. Ben and I made up."

"Don't lie." But she softens her words by making my bathroom walls go a lovely pink.

Setting my phone down, I go to MyHome. Normally, I'd just talk to pull this up, Siri-style, but I'm brushing my teeth at the same time.

"What would you like for breakfast, Sleeping Beauty?" it asks.

On-screen, I select Chex for Kylie. No milk. Though our kitchen is downstairs beside her room, I swear I can hear the robotic arm at work, pouring cereal into the little bowl she still loves, with its chipped image of Elsa from *Frozen*. I select bacon and eggs for Ben, with instructions to cover the plate.

Who knows when he'll roll out of bed?

Kylie interrupts my thoughts with a textalk. "Nothing for me today."

"But I already started cereal," I say as the app now converts talk to text.

"I'll get breakfast on the road. Hail me. K?"

"Fine," I sigh as I picture her commute. So different from my high school days. She's never even driven yet. Using my phone, I order her rideshare. A moving dot appears on my screen showing me that a Chevy Bolt will be here in ten.

My own rideshare gets me thirty minutes later.

Cruising highway I-64 toward Clayton from the western St. Louis suburbs, I'm already hard at work.

"When's it coming?" eighty-nine-year-old Mrs. Henson asks me.

I toggle between my Zoom phone app and the tax refund portal as we teleconverse. Beside us, more professionals like me whiz by in the back seats of other vehicles, talking to their clients or colleagues on their phones. I spot one guy in a suit hosting what looks like a holographic webinar.

"It doesn't say when it's coming, Mrs. Henson," I tell her.

"But it's been *months*, Gena. I go to my mailbox every day. And nothing."

I start to roll my eyes but catch myself, knowing she can see my face. It's times like this that I miss landlines and dumbphones.

"Mrs. Henson, like I said, they stopped mailing checks. You should see it in your account when the payment arrives. Do you have the refund app—"

"I don't know how those things work. *Gerald?*"

Her husband, the one who set up this teleconference, takes over. His hands are shaky, and he doesn't point his camera right, so I only catch glimpses of his lined face.

"Something's wrong with our account," he tells me in a scratchy voice. "I keep getting error messages whenever I try to log on."

For the second time in this conversation, I stop myself from showing annoyance. "That should be an easy fix. Did you try support?"

"You mean them robot things?"

He means AI chatbots, but I don't correct him.

"Why can't we just talk to a live person?" I hear Mrs. Henson say in the background. "Used to be able to drive up to the credit union, and some nice gentleman would help us. Now everything's on your phone. Just awful."

I start to explain it's meant to be more convenient this way, but a text from Ben comes in, distracting me. "So sorry, babe. Let me make it up to you tonight. Dinner and a movie?"

Momentarily forgetting the Hensons, I compose a response text in my head. *Date night's a sweet gesture, but how's that supposed to deal with the underlying issue?*

Just then Mrs. Henson takes the phone from her husband. "Isn't there a way the government can just mail us our check? After all, it *is* our money."

"Of course. There's a procedure for that. Let me walk you through it."

It takes the rest of the office ride to explain to the Hensons how to get paid the old-fashioned way. Several times they stop me to write things down.

"You know, I can just record this conversation on my phone and send it to you," I suggest at one point.

They refuse.

"I'll never figure out how to play that back," says Mrs. Henson.

By the time we pull up to my building, I'm already spent, and the day hasn't begun. My breath steams as the icy January air cuts through my winter coat. It even pierces all those extra layers I piled on. Approaching the outside doors, I catch my driver's reflection in this shiny high-rise on Bemiston Avenue. Tapping on my phone, I pay him for the ride, throwing in a tip.

He politely waves and then backs out into traffic for his next pickup.

"Your health pass, please?" says the robotic voice at the doors.

Behind tempered glass, I catch silhouettes of professionals in the vast foyer. Talking in groups, they make their way toward elevators or the bagel shop with the superb cream cheese and lox I gave up this New Year's.

The little touch screen emitting the sound also displays the same message requesting my health pass. Placing my phone against the panel, I remember when airports began letting passengers use their devices to check in instead of print tickets. That feels like ages ago.

"Inoculations: current," says the voice before scanning begins. An observer watching this would see a red dot on my forehead for a brief second.

And then: "Your temperature falls within normal parameters. Welcome."

Buzz. The electrical locks open.

I enter the building, relaxing as the warmth embraces me.

—

Like every couple, Ben and I met online. Newly divorced from Kylie's father, I was loath to start something new. But Skylar kept bugging me.

"You're pushing fifty. Now's the time to act. Before your window closes."

She said this in the nicest possible way, of course. And it helped that we were sipping proseccos in a Central West End bistro at the time.

At least seeing Ben in real life took the edge off my doubts. Tall and good-looking, he had great eyebrows. They joke about this feature in the classic *Seinfeld* episode where Jerry tries to sell George on a girl he's set him up with.

"Who cares about eyebrows?" George scoffs, inciting the laugh track.

I care about eyebrows. They frame a face, especially in men. And in Ben's case, his accentuated his green eyes, making him appear refined.

It also didn't hurt that he had a good job as a fact-checker.

"They pay me to keep folks honest," he explained. "Lots of misinfo out there."

Unlike me, Ben made his own schedule. A self-confessed night owl, he chose evenings to review articles and videos for objectionable or misleading content. "I can make these folks' lives miserable," he once told me in a burst of pride. "You wouldn't believe the power fact-checkers wield."

That was a couple months ago. In the "salad days," as they call it when couples first hook up. Back then, I had no idea he was the type to throw a wineglass against a wall for the capital offense of meeting up with my ex to attend our reunion together.

"There's nothing there, Ben," I told him. "We just know the same people from high school."

But that wasn't the first time I saw his jealous side. Previous examples included reading my texts (he somehow accessed my phone before it screen-locked) and surveilling my browser history ("What's this site, babe?"); I had to explain I wasn't googling a dentist for any other reason except a teeth cleaning. ("He sure is a *good-looking* dentist.")

Ugh.

And yet, here I am sitting beside him now in the dark watching a rom-com. Holding hands. Munching popcorn. Giggling.

Okay, he's the one laughing.

It's a cheesy flick, but Ben goes for cheesy. We booked our tix online so all we had to do was show the valetbot our phones to enter. Once we settled in, a concessionbot whirred by with drinks we ordered on our phones.

"Just like Puerta Vallarta again. Right, babe? One Corona for you. One for me." Ben pushed the little lime into my bottle before doing the same to his.

Three beers later and twenty minutes into the movie, I felt a little tingle in my jeans pocket. Not wanting to annoy our fellow theatergoers with a blast of cellular light, I sneak a peek to see if it's work.

It's Danny, my ex.

"Who's Ben?" reads his text.

My stomach flips. I've purposely never told Danny anything about my love life. No way would Kylie ever breathe a word, either. She still resents her dad for disappearing on us.

I turn to Ben to confront him, but his eyes are peeled to the big screen. Cuddled this close in our seats, I feel his shoulders convulse with laughter.

I look back at my phone to see Danny has sent a screenshot of a

DM from his Insta. "Thought we should connect since we share Gena in common."

The DM is from Ben's account. *He's stalking me on socials now? WTF.*

"Ben," I whisper in the dark.

An old lady in front of us whips around, bony finger on her lips.

"Yeah, babe?" he whispers back, ignoring the woman.

"Shh," she stage-whispers, swiveling a full 180 degrees, delivering her rebuke with a red-hot stare.

"Nothing," I whisper back.

Because there's nothing left to say. As I watch Ben munch popcorn while swigging beer, all the affection I once had for him pours out in the darkness.

"It's over," I tell him later in the parking lot.

He's not happy, I can tell. He wipes tears from his eyes and stammers about his "plans for us."

"I'm sorry," I say. "This just isn't working for me."

To his credit, Ben gives me a hug before my rideshare arrives. I hug him back, happy to close this chapter of my life.

I sleep better that night than I have in weeks. The problems begin the next morning. Once again, my phone wakes me. Only this time when I try to open Facebook, I'm locked out.

"What the . . . ?"

I check my email. Waiting in my inbox is a form letter alerting me I have violated community standards. "If you feel there's been some mistake, you may file an appeal. It may take up to fourteen days for a response."

I'll do this later, I decide.

It's a Tuesday, and I have back-to-backs scheduled. At least I don't have to worry about disturbing Ben on his side of the bed. Resolved to seize the day with Pilates, I open MyHome to follow along with the AI instructor.

But another error message floods my screen: "Restricted access."

"Um, Mom . . . ?"

Looking up, I see my sixteen-year-old at the door. Backpack slung over her shoulder, Kylie's wet hair is pushed back in a ponytail. "I tried to textalk you, but nothing happened."

"Something's going on, honey. I'm not sure what."

Rolling out of bed, I slip on my robe. Then I flip on the bedroom flatscreen and go into MyHome, expecting to see the familiar words dance across: "What would you like for breakfast, Sleeping Beauty?"

There's nothing of the sort. Just another error message.

"Did you do anything while I was out last night? Change the credit card info?"

Kylie crosses her arms against her chest. "No. You won't tell me your password, remember?"

The morning is a frantic disaster, beginning with the now useless robotic arm in the kitchen. Like a worker on strike, it refuses to cook anything. But since our smartfridge and even our stove is hooked up to MyHome, I can't even manually cook us eggs, much less whip up Kylie's breakfast shake.

"I'll just grab a protein bar," she says, digging into the pantry.

Annoyed, I'm even less prepared to deal with the next crisis. Rideshare won't work either.

"Account suspended," reads the message.

"What?" I all but shriek.

Kylie looks scared. "Mom, what's going on?"

"I honestly don't know." I also have no clue how I will get Kylie to school. "Do they still run school buses?"

"I mean, maybe. Why?"

"'Cause I don't know how else you're gonna get there today."

She sits back down on the living room couch with her protein bar. "I can just log in remotely. That's what other kids do if they're not feeling great and don't want to risk infecting anyone else."

"Good. Do that," I say as I dial up Skylar to ask for a favor.

—

"That's what friends are for. *Honestly*," she tells me as she speeds us over to my office in her Tesla.

Still, I feel bad. "It's your second day. Won't your new boss care?"

She shakes her head, patting me on the shoulder with her manicured nails. "I work remote, remember? It's not like they're logging keystrokes to gauge productivity."

Pulling up outside the big glass-and-steel building, she leans over conspiratorially. By now, she knows the whole sordid tale of Ben and his jealous antics since I described it all in the last twenty minutes. "You know, just because he was a dud doesn't mean you should quit dating altogether."

Peering through her windshield, I see other professionals in coats and gloves queuing up at the doors with their phones to be admitted inside. I notice one lady made the unfortunate decision to wear a dress with no stockings. I shudder imagining how the subzero windchill must feel on her exposed legs.

"That's okay," I tell Skylar. "I'm taking a break from the dating scene."

"For how long?"

"You're happily married. You don't know what it's like out there."

"I wouldn't say *happily*." Then she smiles, revealing that adorable gap between her front teeth I know so well. "But I get it. And I won't push. *Much*."

The display on her dashboard says five minutes to eight. I'd better go.

"Love you." I close the car door behind me. "And thanks again. You're a lifesaver."

The professional crowd is gone when I reach the outside doors. But when I put my phone against the glass, I'm barred from entry. Across the panel, it reads, "Access denied."

No.

Behind me is another professional in my building, a middle-aged guy with graying temples and a leather briefcase.

"Everything okay?" He puts his phone against the wall. It quickly admits him with no issue.

"Would you let me . . . ?" I indicate for him to please let me in too.

He doesn't have to apologize. I can see from the look on his face he's sorry. But he still says no. "They might revoke my lease if word got out."

Bundling up against the cold, I walk and text my clients at the same time to let each know I can't make our meetings today. I don't want to lie, so I keep my rationale vague: "Something came up. Can we reschedule?"

I've contacted them all by the time I reach the little café where I often pop in for a midday scone, especially around tax season. Stomping my feet to remove the snow, I pull the door open, feeling a blast of warm air. The girl at the counter knows me so well she stopped asking for my name on orders.

"Miss Gena," she says brightly. "A mocha, half sweetened?"

"Full sweetened. And a scone. It's been a day."

She nods. "I hear you."

She types in my order and then directs me to place my phone against the pay console. *We've been here before.* I take a deep breath as I place my device against the screen.

"Denied," reads the panel.

Inside I'm screaming, but I keep my voice even. "You take cash?"

She points to a sign that says they do not.

We are the only two people in the café. Outside it's freezing. I don't know where to go or whom to call next.

"Do you mind if I just sit down for a second?"

A flicker of hesitation appears on the barista's young face. It shames me even more than the apologizing guy at the door to my building.

"Sure," she says a second later.

I fall into a table at the back of the café with my head in my hands. That's when I hear the little buzz from my phone.

It's another text from Danny, my ex-husband. "You never got back to me," it reads.

My thoughts are so scrambled that for a second, I cannot remember what he's talking about. Then I scroll up to see his last text and remember what he asked me about last night.

Ben.

With a sickening feeling in my stomach, I recall something Ben told me that first week we started dating—about the power he wields.

"I can make these folks' lives miserable," he once said.

The café door opens, blasting in a gust of cold air.

I shiver, realizing what he's done to me.

TELL

In August 2021, comedian Bill Maher described smartphones. "No other device has ever commanded our constant attention the way a smartphone does," he said in a monologue for his HBO series *Real Time*. "Of course, when I was a teenager, I had a princess phone," he joked. "But I didn't stare at it eight hours a day. There was no hard-core pornography on my family's twenty-four-inch Zenith television set. Sadly." Then he segued into the wider societal implications of this technology. "A former VP at Facebook said he felt tremendous guilt because the short-term, dopamine-driven feedback loops that we have created are destroying how society works."[1]

Maher's point was that Facebook's vice president, Chamath Palihapitiya, was lamenting his role in turning so many of us digital denizens into cyber bullies, Karens, and all-around trolls. Troubling as this development is, smartphones present a more disturbing problem.

They are modern shackles. What's worse? Most of us don't realize it. What's worse than that? We love them.

Let's talk about point number one: Most of us don't realize our bondage. If we zoom past Bill Maher, pop culture can again be counted on to demonstrate the problem—how something this menacing could come to fruition. There is an iconic scene in *The Matrix* where Morpheus (Laurence Fishburne) explains reality to a disbelieving Neo (Keanu Reeves).

"Let me tell you why you're here," says Morpheus. "You're here because you know something. What you know you can't explain, but you feel it. You've felt it your entire life, that there's something wrong with the world. You don't know what it is, but it's there, like a splinter in your mind, driving you mad. It is this feeling that has brought you to me. Do you know what I'm talking about?"

"The Matrix," says Neo.

Only Neo has no clue what this term really means, so Morpheus tells him. "The Matrix is everywhere. It is all around us. Even now, in this very room. You can see it when you look out your window or when you turn on your television. You can feel it when you go to work . . . when you go to church . . . when you pay your taxes. It is the world that has been pulled over your eyes to blind you from the truth."

"What truth?"

"That you are a slave, Neo. Like everyone else, you were born into bondage. Born into a prison that you cannot smell or taste or touch. A prison for your mind."[2]

In many ways, our ubiquitous smartphones are producing an *IRL Matrix*, a prison for our minds—and our bodies. Gena, our protagonist in the above story, experiences this truth for herself. And this speaks to point two: how we love our instruments of oppression.

When her tale begins, Gena is not unlike most of us. She adores the many comforts and conveniences her pocket computer provides:

- A fun conduit to keep up with family and friends
- A helpful communications channel for texting and calling
- A useful taxi-hailing device
- A handy mechanism for payment and entry authorization

Sound familiar? How many of us have come to relish these devices that make life both more convenient and more interesting? Young people have especially come to embrace this tech in hordes. For example, a HuffPost/YouGov survey found that nearly 65 percent of users ages eighteen to twenty-nine admit to falling to sleep with their phone in bed.[3] And that was conducted back in 2013.

It's helpful to quantify in other ways just how much smartphones have taken over the world. *EarthWeb* reports 6.64 billion people now own smartphones globally, including 98 percent of Gen Z.[4] Like Gena, most of us start our day—and end it—by looking at our screens. And according to a *RescueTime* study, people average three hours and fifteen minutes a day on their phones.[5]

An entire book could be written about how so much screen time is wrecking our cognitive functions, turning us into the obnoxious jerks Bill Maher rails about. Though disconcerting, that's not our focus. Instead, we want you to consider how smartphones *already* operate as bondage gadgets—and how they might be further weaponized as ultimate control mechanisms.

Just consider what's happened in the last few years following the COVID-19 pandemic. "With the full rollout of vaccine passports, as seen in Israel, those without a 'green pass' are thrown out of their gyms or choirs and cannot enter many public places," writes Josie Appleton for *Sp!ked*. "In China, those without the Covid 'green code' on their smartphones cannot enter the supermarket or go on the subway."[6]

Oblivious to such concerns, Gena, our story's stand-in for every privileged middle-class person, had her world rocked when suddenly that very smartphone she so loved turned on her. No longer a tool for technological convenience, it shackled her the moment she "stepped out of line."

But let's pause here to make a key distinction.

If you'll recall, Gena didn't do anything nefarious to warrant her oppression. She just happened to date a jealous guy with the power to ruin her life. Such arbitrariness presents the real danger of centralization. What happens when other less than scrupulous authorities possess such control over us?

Until recently, it was quite difficult for even the most repressive regimes to restrict and restrain people at scale. There were ways around the system.

But nowadays and under the new control grid abetted by the smartphone, there's nowhere to run. Not only do our little pocket devices always know precisely where we are (even when they are shut off), but they can also be used as virtual prison bars. They can restrict our participation in society in ways little different from a locked-up convict denied their freedom.

So how did we get here?

History offers a guide. In the twentieth century, totalitarian governments became more sophisticated in how they denied liberty to their people. Inspired by the likes of Nazi propagandist Joseph Goebbels and marketer Edward Bernays, who wrote the book *Propaganda* in 1928, they updated their control methods. They grokked that it's far easier to subdue populations via controlling information than by employing brute force. Why bother with bullets and batons when you can gain submission through more sophisticated and less harmful means?

The twenty-first-century upgrade works even better.

It takes little convincing to produce a nation—or world—of Genas. Could anything be better than our devices possessing a million times more computing power than the Apollo 11 mission? Gena sure wouldn't have thought so.

Not until she lost everything.

Like Gena, we adore our smartphones. We love the convenience. We thrill at the latest app. We relish streaming movies and TV on demand. And, of course, we're addicted to all those serotonin hits we get each time someone texts us, likes our post, comments on it, or reshares it on social media.

Transfixed by our glowing screens—all those shiny lights, all those beeping, buzzing sounds—have we fallen into the totalitarian trap? Have we sleepwalked right into an invisible prison for our minds and our bodies?

Ask Gena.

2

~~MINISTRY~~ MONOPOLY

OF TRUTH

SHOW

This is unbelievable. I can't believe this crap.

Danny pushed down the volume of the voice blasting in his head to better hear Mrs. Warren, his teacher sporting platinum helmet hair. "And over here we can see Stonyside's first soda fountain. Just as it looked in 1955."

Twenty-eight eighth graders on the field trip turned to look where she pointed. Before their eyes, an empty parking lot filled with strewn litter became a café.

And not just any diner. It burst to life as a brightly lit soda shop with hot turquoise and pink neon lights. At one corner of a checkered floor, a wooden cabinet jukebox blasted Chuck Berry's "Roll Over Beethoven" from a 45 record.

That's it. That's the goddamn place. Gives me chills.

Danny looked on at the café as a familiar but painful weight settled in the pit of his stomach. Ignoring it, he watched as holographic high schoolers in cardigans and corduroys ignored rows of barstools lining the counters. Instead, they were on their feet, bopping to the music, clapping, and twirling around the room with breathless energy. Both White and Black kids.

Nice little fantasy we got us here.

The joyful scene affected Danny's classmates. Buoyed by the old-fashioned music, some began to nod their heads to the beat.

Danny had a different reaction. It made him sick.

Mrs. Warren cleared her throat, and a second later the rock 'n' roll ditty became softer, as though someone had turned down the volume with a TV remote.

"Who here knows what an apothecary is?" she asked the class.

A lone hand went up. It belonged to Anna. Even before she rattled off her answer in that singsongy voice of hers, Danny could see collective eyes roll.

"Um, an apothecary is like a pharmacy. You know, like a CVS where your mom and dad go to get a prescription."

"Good," said Mrs. Warren. "Now, what you're all too young to know is that in the beginning of the last century, we didn't have places like CVS on every street corner. Cafés like the one you see here served as *drugstore fountains.*"

"Why were they all dancing then?" asked Kendall, the boy beside Danny with long bangs spilling into his eyes.

"Good question. To answer it, you need to know more history. Soda fountains began with what's called the drug revolution in the 1850s. Back then, parents would go to their local drugstore to get their fountain drink containing all types of medicines, even SSRIs for children with attention deficit."

Oh my word.

"Kids used to get their meds from a fountain drink?" another boy asked.

Mrs. Warren nodded. "I know it sounds silly now, but people didn't think the same way we did back then. Many of the fountain drinks were really medical concoctions but sweetly flavored so they didn't taste gross."

"I heard they had cocaine in them," whispered the tall girl beside Danny.

"That's true," said Mrs. Warren. "But like I said, this was a long time ago, so people didn't know as much about the science."

Science, my chapped ass.

"Anyway, it so happened that cafés like the one you see here became the backbone of Main Street USA. And by the time the 1950s rolled around, they were also places for social gatherings. Don't they look like they're having fun?"

Danny's face soured on that last word.

Fun. If that's what you want to call it.

Anna raised her hand. "But I heard that Blacks and Whites were segregated in those days. Like they had separate bathrooms and stuff."

Danny whipped his head around to stare at Anna.

Finally. Let's see what the old crone has to say about that.

"Not sure where you heard that, but it's not true." The smile on Mrs. Warren's face stayed plastered in place. "In fact, Stonyside elected its first Black mayor—a queer one at that—just the year prior."

God in heaven! She can't be serious.

Mrs. Warren continued, "The place you see here was called Molly's Café, and it closed on May 5, 1951, when developers bought the parcel and the land around it to convert it into the town's flagship savings and loan."

The moment she said that, the café morphed before their eyes. The song stopped, and the dancing teens vanished, along with the café. A much larger, square building replaced it. Danny's class could see into the first floor where people of all races in suits and ties waited on customers behind wooden stalls.

Danny watched as a White woman with a stroller approached a bank teller.

Like hell this happened.

"While it certainly doesn't look like as much fun as that diner, this bank served as a pillar of Stonyside commerce until well into the twenty-first century," said Mrs. Warren as she pointed to the VR scene behind her. All the holographic people looked indistinguishable from anyone you might meet on the street.

Uh-uh. There was never any bank there. A liquor store . . . ? Yes. Right after they bulldozed Molly's.

Danny wanted to lie down. Maybe that would stop the horrible weight in his stomach from dragging him under the earth. But he held it together.

"What's that weird paper she's giving him?" asked Kendall, the blond boy with the surfer look, indicating the White woman at the teller counter.

Mrs. Warren chuckled. "Oh, that's an old-fashioned check. People used them before the One-Government secured the banking system. Watch what happens next."

The woman held out her hand for the teller to hand her cash. Instead, he shook his head. A minute later, two Black police officers in uniforms surrounded the woman from either side.

"I'm afraid your check is fraudulent," said one of the officers. "You're under arrest."

Say something, boy. You have to.

Danny opened his mouth—and promptly closed it. He didn't want to risk a demerit. Or worse.

But the woman with the stroller wasn't about to go quietly. She resisted the cops trying to handcuff her. "Get your hands off me! I have rights."

When they wouldn't let go, she pulled a pistol from her bag. Before she could point it, the police subdued her with an electromagnetic pulse ray. She didn't seem to suffer as she slumped to the floor beside her stroller.

That was when Mrs. Warren froze the frame to address her class. "As you can also see, America back then was an extremely violent place."

"Even mothers used guns back then?" asked Kendall.

"Yes. Even them. The One-Gov outlawed all firearms in the landmark 2030 Gun Treaty precisely because of commonplace incidents like this."

That's not at all what happened, and you know it, you witch.

"Okay. Moving on."

Mrs. Warren led the class down Truman Street. The moment they stepped away from the scene, the bank melted into the deserted parking lot.

Several hundred feet later, they stopped again, this time before an electric refueling station. Since it was a familiar sight to the kids from Stonyside Middle, they took little notice of the spindly robotic arms latching on to self-driving vehicles before propelling them toward their cubicles. Once docked, they automatically began renewing the cars' batteries through conduction.

"This is the harder part of our tour," began Mrs. Warren. As she spoke, the filling station morphed into a weather-beaten building made of brick. A skeleton-like fire escape stuck out of one side like a broken femur. Cheap, thin TV antennas protruded from the roof, reflecting a beating sun.

"Probably some of you have family members who are journalists. Have you ever stopped to ask why they need licenses?"

Oh. Here we go with this crap.

No one raised their hand. Not even Anna knew why. Danny did, but he knew better than to answer. He was already on thin ice this semester.

"No one has a guess?" asked Mrs. Warren. "Well, before the Truth in Media Law passed a few years back, dishonest reporters and even whole media companies would propagandize people."

"What's propaganda?" asked one of Danny's classmates.

'Course you don't know that word.

"Fake news. Lies. Corrupt journalists could make up anything they liked. Anything at all. Even if it was misinformation."

"But misinfo can get people hurt or even killed, Mrs. Warren," said Anna, her arms crossed. "Why would they do that?"

As Mrs. Warren approached the young woman, her voice took on a softer tone. "Sorry to trigger you. Honestly, it was a different time. Remember how we learned about the Wild West? How lawlessness reigned until people passed laws to protect the innocent townspeople and Native Americans?"

"Yes," said a stiffened Anna.

"This was a lot like that. It was dangerous. To protect the public, lawmakers passed legislation so bad journalists wouldn't ever be able to manipulate people again."

If you kids only knew.

Anna relaxed. "I'm glad they did that, Mrs. Warren."

"Me too." As they moved away from the retired news building, it morphed back into the electric fueling station. Since Mrs. Warren had been speaking, most of the vehicles had finished charging and were now off to pick up their passengers. "We have one more stop on our tour; then we'll call it a day."

I don't know if I can do this. I don't know if I can see it again.

But Danny trudged forward along with his classmates.

They passed by high-rise mixed-use skyscrapers with smart tech–enabling plants on the rooftops to reposition themselves to best receive the sun's rays. Danny looked up to see misting drones gently watering them. A faint rainbow emerged between the aqua spray.

Stopping to watch the beautiful prism of colors forming, he didn't feel that horrible heaviness, for the first time all day.

"Come along, Danny," Mrs. Warren said. "We're waiting."

Here we go.

Danny looked up to see that he was in the back of the line. Switching to a jog, he caught up to the others as they rounded the corner before the graveyard. Danny and his classmates took their places, standing in a vast, sloping lawn with blossoming azaleas. Cracked tombstones in disrepair poked through the ground like growing teeth.

Turn back. Just turn back. Let's not do this.

Danny backed away from the others listening intently to Mrs. Warren. As she recited historical facts about the war that produced so many of these graves, he pondered the ancient oak trees. Though new to Stonyside, he thought he could somehow find the infamous branch.

Cupping his hand over his brow to reduce the midday glare, he kept his eyes on the trees. A ghastly vision, the result of all those stories, leaped into his head. He saw the rope swaying. Lifeless eyes. Dark skin caked in blood.

Mrs. Warren's voice cut through his grim reverie. "Stonyside Memorial officially closed in 1949, two years after World War II. There hasn't been a burial here since—"

"What about burying someone alive?"

Everyone turned to Danny in surprise.

"What are you talking about?" asked Mrs. Warren.

He wished he hadn't said anything. He wanted to disappear.

Keep going. Keep going.

All twenty-eight of his classmates now openly stared at Danny. The heaviness in his stomach had gone full tilt. If he didn't find something to lean against soon, he would collapse.

Keep going. Keep going. Tell them what really happened.

"Danny?" asked Mrs. Warren. Her plastered smile was back.

The iron fence wasn't so far away. Danny wondered if he could make it.

Tell them. For me. For her!

"Mrs. Warren." Danny wobbled on unsteady feet. "Molly's didn't let in Black people back in the '50s. Especially not to dance beside Whites."

Mrs. Warren's smile stayed in place. "And how would you know that?"

"There was a night. A terrible night. My great-grandfather worked in the kitchen as a dishwasher. Someone made a comment to his wife just as they were leaving—"

"All right. No more silly fairy tales. Thank you very much, Danny."

Danny pressed on. "It was a White guy and some friends. They grabbed him before he made it to his car. They tortured my papa—"

Still smiling, Mrs. Warren was losing her patience. "Okay, I said stop."

"They strapped him to their bumper and then drug him all the way here—"

"Enough!"

"Strung him up in the tree and made him watch as they buried her. She was still breathing—"

"Stop!"

"When they covered her in dirt . . ."

All his classmates gaped at Danny, who now lay crumpled on the ground, clutching his stomach. Mrs. Warren had recovered her smile. She used it on Danny as she approached. "We value your truth. Thank you for sharing. Now if you'll please stand up, we will resume our field trip."

The second Danny stood, the Stonyside Middle server disconnected him from the Metaverse. He found himself back in his family's small apartment dressed in his school-issued VR haptic suit.

Tears filled his eyes as he looked up at his papa. The latter had been witnessing everything in real time on their monitor.

"I shouldn't have put you through that," he croaked in a broken voice.

It matched his broken body, with its maze of scars and his one working eye in a wrinkled socket.

"No, Papa. I wanted to know our history. What really happened."

"Then it's time you read about it too."

Papa limped to the desk and opened a drawer. Inside were old newspaper clippings so brittle they nearly flaked off as he unfolded one. Danny could see the faded picture of a beautiful young Black woman.

"What a smile your great-grandmother had. She sure would've loved to meet you, Danny."

TELL

In 2021, *Ahrefs* ranked Wikipedia as the number-one most-visited website on the internet in the United States and third worldwide. In America, it outpaced Amazon, Facebook, even pornographic sites. The editors arrived at their determination through accessing monthly organic traffic.[1]

That's a lot of eyeballs, to put it lightly. That's also a lot of power.

It's a good bet you often use Wikipedia, or what's now called the "definitive digital encyclopedia," to research topics, learn about various subjects, or gather statistics. Right now, it possesses nearly ten million entries and receives hundreds of millions of visits daily. Just as Google has become synonymous with search, the popular site is the go-to knowledge compendium.

"Well," you might ask, "what's so bad about that?"

For starters, it's dangerous to centralize all knowledge in one entity. Or suggest that one entity can be trusted to be the main knowledge authority. That's too much power. And we know what happens when power accumulates.

The late Lord Acton warned us about this threat in the nineteenth century with these immortal words: "Power tends to corrupt and absolute power corrupts absolutely. Great men are almost always bad men, even when they exercise influence and not authority: still more when you superadd the tendency or the certainty of corruption by authority."[2]

Likewise, novelist George Orwell predicted the totalitarian threat when those in charge designate one body as the supreme informational authority. In his dystopian masterpiece *1984*, he labels it "the Ministry of Truth."[3]

Unlike Wikipedia, this entity has a physical presence in his book. Clocking in at three hundred meters and possessing three thousand rooms, it's devoted not to the pursuit of facts but, rather, to propaganda.

Orwell's protagonist, Winston Smith, works for the Party in the "Records Department." Here his activities include changing historical documents to best present Big Brother (a.k.a. the government). Other Ministry of Truth branches engage in similar forms of deception. They do so by producing mass media for education and entertainment via altering, updating, or outright deleting news, books, films, and articles. "The Party told you to reject the evidence of your eyes and ears. It was their final, most essential command," Orwell wrote.[4]

Nightmarish as Orwell's vision is, he *understates* the problem in *1984*. You see, his novel was published in 1949 before widespread computer usage. Prescient as he was, Orwell worried about the *physical* alteration and manipulation of content. Now that we have digital files, it's easier to control information flow in real time and, in the process, affect even more people more quickly.

To appreciate the problem, think about how definitions of words have changed in recent years. Writing for *Forbes* in 2009, author and researcher Michael Fumento decried how the World Health Organization changed its definition of the word *pandemic* during the H1N1 outbreak:

> Medically, the pandemic moniker is unjustifiable. When the sacrosanct World Health Organization (WHO) made its official declaration in June, we were 11 weeks into the outbreak, and swine flu had only killed 144 people worldwide. . . . So how could WHO make such an outrageous claim? Simple. It rewrote the definition of "pandemic."[5]

Here's another example. In June 2020, the WHO's definition of *herd immunity* read as follows: "Herd immunity is the indirect protection from an infectious disease that happens when a population is immune either through vaccination or immunity developed through previous infection."[6]

Today, the World Health Organization also includes the following sentence after its current definition: "WHO supports achieving 'herd immunity' through vaccination, not by allowing a disease to spread through any segment of the population, as this would result in unnecessary cases and deaths."[7] Also, there is a link to the director-general's opening remarks at an October 12, 2020, media briefing supporting the updated definition of herd immunity:

> There has been some discussion recently about the concept of reaching
> so-called "herd immunity" by letting the virus spread.
>
> Herd immunity is a concept used for vaccination, in which a popu-
> lation can be protected from a certain virus if a threshold of vaccination
> is reached.
>
> For example, herd immunity against measles requires about 95% of
> a population to be vaccinated. The remaining 5% will be protected by the
> fact that measles will not spread among those who are vaccinated.
>
> For polio, the threshold is about 80%.[8]

In other words, herd immunity is achieved by protecting people
from a virus, not by exposing them to it. Extrapolating, it's easy to imagine how the truth can be distorted when online content can be updated
in real time with little or no input or verification from the public. Not
long ago, it was hard to change the definitions of words.

That was before Wikipedia and the widespread usage of digital
content.

Of course, Wikipedia is emblematic of our fast-paced times. It
offers instant information to people hungry for knowledge on every
conceivable topic—a public that's used to and expects instant gratifica-
tion, including "the facts." Once upon a time, *Encyclopedia Britannica*
salespeople sold you their heavy books door-to-door. Back then entries
depended on the insights of highly researched and scholarly experts
who might spend years researching a topic.

No more. "Experts" you've never heard of are suddenly bastions of
trust with a monopoly on truth.

Of course, Wikipedia pays lip service to safeguards. Here's a statement from its own site concerning its policy on verifiability: "In the
English Wikipedia, *verifiability* means other people using the encyclopedia can check that the information comes from a reliable source.
Wikipedia does not publish original research. Its content is determined by previously published information rather than the beliefs or

experiences of editors. Even if you are sure something is true, it must be verifiable before you can add it. If reliable sources disagree, then maintain a neutral point of view and present what the various sources say, giving each side its due weight."[9]

On its face, this sounds like a perfectly reasonable defense of Wikipedia's verification policies. Until we ask pointed questions.

Here a few:

- What is a "reliable source"?
- What if the "previously published information" is false or misleading?
- What makes information "verifiable"?
- Who determines what qualifies as a "neutral point of view"?
- Who determines what "various sources" are acceptable?
- When it comes to "giving each side its due weight," who determines the "sides," and who decides they have been given "due weight"?

Former *New York Times* journalist Chris Hedges raised alarms about Wikipedia back in October 2018 on the now defunct news series *On Contact* for RT.[10] (It should be noted that the video in question has since been scrubbed from most of the web, making it difficult to find. Also, because of the Russian-Ukrainian war, RT has been censored in the UK. Both these developments cut to the core of the centralization problem we are discussing.)

In the episode, Hedges interviews investigative journalist Helen Buyniski about how Wikipedia serves as a "tool of the ruling elite." According to Buyniski, the site is perceived to be the "holy oracle of truth, but it's anything but." We are also meant to believe it's the product of one hundred thousand unpaid volunteers "with open access," working to share their knowledge as experts.[11]

In reality? It's a top-down organization that gets to determine what's real or not from on high. "As these things start to calcify, a sort of hierarchy takes place so that Wikipedia is not just egalitarian," says Buyniski. "There are administrators, a sort of Supreme Court and an arbitration committee. . . . It just becomes vying factions of power where the people at the top don't want to let the people at the bottom do what they want."[12]

Sounds a lot like the Ministry of Truth, where ruling authorities get to determine reality. As just one more example of the problem, nearly all of Buyniski's investigative pieces on Wikipedia no longer appear online. They simply don't exist. (Kind of like a real-life Winston Smith disappeared them.)

After hours of combing, we did find this entry from Buyniski that sums up the issue: "Our in-depth investigation has found that everything we've been led to believe about Wikipedia is a lie. . . . Scratch the surface of the 'free encyclopedia anyone can edit' and you find a finely-honed propaganda machine manipulated by experts and used to destroy the reputations of those who dare question the status quo."[13]

That last point has resonance. If you happen to be a public figure, you probably know you're not in full control of your Wikipedia page. So-called third-party editors or volunteers often get to decide what the public knows about you.

And what if they get it wrong? If you're a writer with a following, what if they accuse you of some heinous crime like plagiarism?

This is what happened to Chris Hedges, the same reporter who dared to challenge Wikipedia. For years Wikipedia called out plagiarism accusations against him, under the heading "Allegation of Plagiarism," on its site just because Christopher Ketchum of the *New Republic* asserted them.[14]

Forget about the Constitution's presumption of innocence until proven guilty. Anyone in the years 2014–2018 who looked Hedges up on the web's most heavily trafficked site would be informed that Hedges is a plagiarist, indicting him in the court of public opinion.

It's hard to live a bad reputation down. It's worse if the bad perception is undeserved. Is this the kind of fear we want to live with when centralized knowledge behemoths dictate what construes our consensus reality?

But even this description, bad as it is, understates the problem.

Right now, people can access Wikipedia and other sites claiming a monopoly on truth from *two-dimensional* screens such as monitors, tablets, and phones. And already, we can see the power they wield. It's leviathan—the kind of force capable of ruining careers and even taking down governments.

It will get much worse with the arrival of the metaverse.

For context, let's recall that Facebook CEO Mark Zuckerberg did not coin this term. "The virtual world where people will live, work, and play" began as a futuristic idea—back in 1992. That year, sci-fi writer Neal Stephenson published the book *Snow Crash*. It predicted a dystopia in which the global economy has crashed along with the federal government. Only a handful of uber rich corporations hold sway over what's left of the United States we once knew.

Columnist Tom Huddleston Jr., writing for CNBC, can fill in some other plot details: "The metaverse is an escape, and the novel's main character—a nearly broke computer hacker and pizza delivery driver who bears a tongue-in-cheek name, Hiro Protagonist—spends much of his time there. He accesses the metaverse by wearing goggles and 'earphones,' and appears within the digital world as his own customized avatar. Once there, avatars can stroll down a single wide street, tens of thousands of miles long, and home to amusement parks, shops, offices, and entertainment complexes."[15]

Sounds a lot like the virtual (alternate) reality Zuckerberg wants to unleash in the coming years. Already, middle schoolers (not to mention high schoolers and elementary school–aged children) the same age as Danny spend much of their waking lives staring at screens, divorced from reality. Can we imagine what will happen when the web goes *three-dimensional*—when all it takes is a haptic suit and goggles to jack into the net—so we can live, work, and play?

For one thing, we can expect Wikipedia and other informational gatekeepers to assume centralized powers dwarfing any hellscape Orwell could dream up. The make-believe field trip Danny and his classmates go on—and the lies they are force-fed—present just the tip of the iceberg as to what's possible under such tyranny.

After all, seeing is believing. And it's possible to supercharge that *believing* by packing on additional sensorial layers.

In our story, Danny and the other kids don't simply read about recent history. They get to experience it by being placed in the narrative, reliving events with holographic avatars so lifelike they feel as real as the physical three-dimensional universe we now inhabit.

Knowing that people are social creatures and highly suggestible, it takes little imagination to conceive of a not-so-distant time where less than scrupulous historians, educators, and other authorities literally rewrite history. Then force us to experience it. And believe it.

Of course, it doesn't take unscrupulous individuals to bring about this degradation of consensual reality. Wikipedia and other gatekeeper sites aren't created and managed by evil manipulators wishing to distort the truth. Instead, they are made up of regular people like you and me. People with biases and prejudices. People who also hold agendas and lack full understandings.

In short, it's a very human endeavor prone to human mistakes.

The error we make is to forget this point. It's not that Wikipedia should be dissolved or destroyed. Rather, we should acknowledge the benefit of a *plurality* of opinions and ideas. As Lord Acton told us, "Power corrupts. And absolute power corrupts absolutely."[16]

Possessing too much centralized power, especially in the form of information, is a recipe for a totalitarian disaster the likes of which we have never seen.

"History is written by the victors," goes the aphorism. There's truth to it. Dictators from Joseph Stalin to Saddam Hussein knew what they were doing when they changed the schoolbooks children of their regimes were allowed to read. Lenin is commonly quoted as saying, "Give me four years to teach the children, and the seed I have sown will never be uprooted."

Can you appreciate what rotten trees we shall produce in the years to come if we do not rise up against our own ~~ministries~~ monopolies of truth?

3

THE COMPANY LINE

SHOW

"Here, let me."

Denise wraps her arms around my neck like she so often did during all those long working years. Inhaling her sweet lilac perfume, I relax, letting her complete our ritual decades in the making.

"There. *Perfect.*" She steps back so we can both admire her handiwork in our bedroom mirror.

That's when Amber bursts in with little Spence. "Aw, you two are so cute. Just like that elderly couple in *Grumpy Old Men*. Still hot for each other."

"Ha," Denise snorts, pulling away in her black evening gown. "Your father just keeps me around 'cause he never learned to tie a tie."

My secret. If it were a few decades ago, I'd never let the truth out. How she would smuggle three or four pre-tied ties into my bag before

I hit the road so all I had to do was tighten them at the neck before meetings.

That was a long time ago.

Say what you will about getting old, but the passage of time has its perks. Life's stings lose their venom. You stop caring so much what everyone thinks.

Picking up my five-year-old grandson, we touch noses Eskimo-style.

"When we going to your birthday?" little Spence asks, still in my arms.

I chuckle, and Amber cuts in. "It's not Grandpa's *birthday*. It's his retirement party. And you're not going. You have a babysitter."

"Correction. It's also our bon voyage party," says Denise, drinking from a champagne flute.

She puts her arms around me again. Though I won't claim psychic powers, she and I have known each other so long that we telegraph thoughts. Right now, her mind is on the next fourteen days. "Our honeymoon do-over," she calls it.

"Did Bethany ever text you?" Denise asks. "She was supposed to be at the restaurant setting up but said there was a problem with the cake."

I retrieve my phone from my pocket. There's no message from my other daughter. Instead, I see the little alert that raises my blood pressure. Five stars are nearly all grayed out.

"Something the matter?" asks Denise.

"Not at all," I lie. "Just jitters at seeing everyone from my past life."

"You shouldn't be. You outdid everyone's expectations. How many of your peers can say they took a risk like you?"

She means Hawthorne Thorpe and the late-stage career gamble I'm beginning to wish I never took. The problems all began with a stupid joke. Or rather a jokey email. My client Bob sent me a one-sentence email: "Hey, Theo. Just saw nickel is through the roof. I should fire you for not telling me sooner!"

Ha-ha, Bob.

That's just his personality. If you met the scrappy eighty-six-year-old in person (it would have to be at his club, and you would have to be drinking an old-fashioned with him), you'd pick up on his wry wit.

You'd know the man couldn't possibly be serious about his comment. Only AIs don't joke. And they sure don't understand humor.

But try telling that to the ghouls of Hawthorne Thorpe. For starters, you'd be hard-pressed to *reach* the ghouls. First they offshored their service reps to India. Then they onshored them when they demanded bigger salaries.

Not about to cut into their own profits, Hawthorne management hit on another tack: Robo-source it all. Let customers and vendors alike go through AIs for everything: AIs to answer your investing queries, AIs to handle transfers, and now AIs to *spy on its financial advisors to ensure compliance?*

Before I tell you about Bob and his joke that sicced the AIs on me, I must digress. I came up in a world where you clocked in at nine and left at five, an era where you worked for the same company year after year. There was no such thing as the "gig economy."

My generation was full of lifers like me. Company men. And later, women. We didn't have HR back then breathing down our backs or any of the many rules they have today. *Compliance*, they call it now. What is "compliance"? Seems to me the real definition is "obey." Next time someone tells you, "I'm with compliance," what they really mean is "I'm here to make sure you submit."

Anyhow, the real trouble started last year.

Before that I was a company man with SAS Brokerage. That's where I cut my teeth forty years ago. I put in the time building my book there, beginning with selling family members life insurance. Not an easy thing to do, as any advisor will tell you. "Hey, Uncle Todd. Ever thought what might happen to Aunt Sheila if, God forbid, you were to pass away?"

That's not a conversation I ever want to have again.

As my hair thinned and my belly swelled, I amassed more than three hundred clients. Not just in Tampa, either. Back then, I was on the road forty weeks of the year, Denise's pre-tied ties neatly stowed in my bag. No Zoom teleconferences for us old-timers. I stayed in motels, putting on wealth management workshops for rotary clubs, teaching working stiffs how to prepare for retirement so it didn't sucker punch them in old age. "Failing to plan is planning to fail," I'd say.

It wasn't a bad gig, either.

All that grinding paid Denise's and my mortgage. It put our daughters, Bethany and Amber, through nursing school. Because of it, we enjoyed Christmases in Maui every two years, and even now it affords me enough to make monthly contributions to little Spence's 529. Unlike me, fifteen years from now, he can expect to go to college.

But that's not all. Tonight, I have another surprise for him. Okay, for his mom. Wait 'til I tell her and Denise and everyone else at the party that all those years of saving paid off.

No "staycation" honeymoon for future Spencer. Not if I can help it.

I finish Eskimo-kissing the little boy I adore and slip his babysitter another ten on the way out. "If you take good care of my grandson," I tell the teen girl with glasses and the ponytail, "there's another couple of those waiting for you." She smiles before leading little Spence off to play with his blocks.

As Amber drives her mom and me to the restaurant for tonight's shindig, I stare out the window at passing split-level houses dotting the Floridian coast. Along with weedy palm trees, they whip past us in the waning afternoon light. Rolling down the window, I suck in the balmy air, reflecting on time's passage.

"You're the hardest working man I ever met," Dell, my first boss at SAS, once told me. "Like a man possessed."

If he only understood why. I never told him, though. Back then shame was my copilot. Or maybe my driver. Over the years it steered me toward competency. I got good at selling a range of financial products: 401(k)s, Roth and traditional IRAs, SEPs, mutual funds, bonds, stocks, you name it.

"Your clients just love you," Dell would remark.

The proof was in the pudding. Each December, Denise and I ran out of space on the mantle to house all the holiday cards we received. I went to endless holiday parties. Weddings of my clients' kids. Their Bar Mitzvahs. And occasionally, funerals. The people I served thought of me like family. Before it became an industry buzzword, I really was their trusted advisor.

I did so well, in fact, that I made a dumb mistake a year ago.

Call it pride, call it ego, but I thought I could be like all those other entrepreneurs I helped along. Seeking to break away from all that corporateness that about drove me batty, I decided to establish my own financial consultancy.

Sayonara, Compliance, I thought. *You don't own me. I'm my own man.*

Easier said than done. Turns out I still required the backing of a major wealth management player to underwrite my new firm. That's where Hawthorne Thorpe came in, a vast diversified entity with billions in holdings, boasting AAA ratings.

Oh well, I thought, *at least I can bring my own clients over when I put out my shingle.*

In retrospect, that was the only silver lining. To my horror, Hawthorne was one thousand times worse when it came to compliance. The difference is that their gatekeepers weren't people. They were AIs. I'm talking about artificial intelligence bots straight out of *The Twilight Zone*.

And apparently, it was Bob's stupid email that first put me in their crosshairs. Minutes after I called the old lout to tell him I did indeed recommend metals in my annual review to stave off inflationary pain—I got what's called a *ping* from the AI surveillance bots.

"Please be advised, Mr. Wilson," began the tactful censure in my inbox, "we at Hawthorne Thorpe believe in encouraging mutually beneficial relationships between our wealth advisors and clients—" I skipped to the point. "Any time we detect a less than harmonious exchange, it's incumbent upon our organization to bring it to your attention. It is our sincere hope that you will see this as an opportunity to provide greater benefit to those you serve."

Translation: The bots were snooping on my emails via the company server. I thought about firing back an email: "Hey, you KGB agents, I can handle my own business. Thanks, but buzz off."

Maybe I should've sent that, because things slid downhill from there. Weeks later, I sent an email to a different client. Nothing out of the ordinary, mind you. It was the usual language I include when rolling over a 401(k).

But the bots must have been on to me, because right afterward I got another pushy email. This one was written in the same polite compliance speak: "Today's investor isn't solely driven by ROI metrics. They want to know that their investments complement their life's purpose. Learn how you can change the conversation from money to meaning."

Whatever you say. Ignoring the unsolicited advice, I went about my day.

I thought little of the message because I was so busy on my project: moving earnings into the money market account I had established for little Spence. It was set up before he was born, and I hadn't told his mom yet, or even Denise. All those years at SAS, I'd watched my savvier clients, learning how they made moves. Instead of pouring money into a second home like my friends or buying a fancy car, I spent excess money this way, quarter after quarter. Building a nest egg. The kind my mom and I could have used.

Things were so quiet from the Hawthorne side for a few weeks that I nearly forgot about the bots. That is, until a message popped up minutes before I was to meet with the Delaneys, a new client.

"Be sure to suggest the Purpose Pact," it read. "It's a sustainable and inclusive way to mindfully invest." Embedded in the email was an offer to have the Delaneys complete what they dubbed a Purpose Predictor online. "By answering ten survey questions, we at Hawthorne can generate a Purpose Profile, detailing goals and missions aligned with your client's values."

I read on.

According to the message, once the questionnaire "identified" what causes mattered most to the Delaneys, the bots would pick designated public companies for investment. Or as Hawthorne explained, "We choose those organizations committed to the highest level of stakeholder return."

Who gives a flip? I thought. *The Delaneys just want to make sure they've got enough in the bank to retire.* Reading this garbage made me want a cigarette. And I haven't smoked since little Spence was born.

—

My computer monitor chimes, letting me know the Delaneys have entered my personal chat room. Minimizing my email tab, I throw my attention into meeting with this new couple. In their early thirties, they seem like sweet kids. Andy, the husband, works for a boutique mortgage brokerage. His wife, Kara, is six weeks away from delivering their first child. She plans to take off for a few years to be with the baby. I applaud their choice. It's what Denise and I did, though it sure wasn't easy.

When I finish the teleconference, I feel better than I have in days. People think financial advisors are only in it for the money. Maybe some are. But that's not what got me out of bed all those mornings when we were struggling.

I could've done other stuff. Laid brick like my brother-in-law. Gone back to teaching PE. No, I did this because I like helping people. It's a great feeling to know you're setting up some youngsters for life. My old man croaked when I was ten, leaving me nothing but half-drunk bottles of Jack. For Mom? The unwelcome surprise of pissed-off creditors demanding payment.

Tunneling our way out of that mudslide cut Mom's life short and made me hate the man. I refused to say his name most of my adulthood. Shame can do that to you. The humiliation of wanting to take your new wife to Venice like she always dreamed—but going nowhere so you can afford your mortgage.

How money haunted me back then. Lying in bed at 2:00 a.m., I could hear Denise breathing, the new baby snuggled into the crook of her arm. That's when I'd run a balance sheet through my head, divvying what we owed, what was owed to us.

Then came the night of Davis Peterson's retirement party.

Davis had been my client for years, and the assembled crowd consisted of men like him: blue-collar guys who had worked in the same car plant for decades. I must have been about Andy Delaney's age then. Sitting in that smoky back room of some Italian restaurant, I watched all those codgers sucking down their cigars as they threw back whiskey.

"If I'd known it all would've flown by so fast, I wouldn't have let it get to me so much," Davis said. He paused to dab his eyes. To my amazement, he didn't look ashamed. "I guess I woulda enjoyed the ride more."

After that, I vowed not to let the same things get to me either. I stopped fearing life's balance sheet, the losses and the wins. I also forgave Dad. In the coming years, Davis stayed on my mind as I shifted my firm's focus. I made it my mission to set up young people for success so they also wouldn't fear the future—so they would be set up in their golden years. Unlike Mom.

—

Ping.

A week before my retirement party, an alert floats across my screen. It features the Hawthorne logo of a tree with roots extending into soil. "Your performance score is in jeopardy," it reads. Beside the words, I see five stars like an Amazon review. Three stars are grayed, indicating my rating of 2.5.

The hell? Until this second, I didn't know there was *a grading system.*

On impulse I pick up my phone to call someone at Hawthorne. Then I remember the last time I tried to ring customer service. It was like a Kafka novel. Layers and layers of automated recordings kept me in some endless phone maze until I couldn't stand it anymore and hung up.

So instead, I type a note to the little Hawthorne bot with the cheery tree icon who always hovers on my browser. "Can you tell me what I did wrong?"

"I am not sure what you mean by your question," it shoots back. "You may choose from our menu of options. Would you like to discuss investment strategies? ETFs? Market volatility? How about Hawthorne's commitment to green investing?"

Thank God no one is around because I literally scream in exasperation. That cigarette is sounding better and better by the second.

"Why did my performance score drop?" I type.

Instead of a written response, the bot drops in a hyperlink. It takes me to a policy page on Hawthorne's site. Somewhere in a jungle of legalese I find this curious statement: "Brokerage associates agree to our terms of conditions. Those who don't adhere to our standards may be subject to penalties."

What does that mean?

All the rest of that week I am on pins and needles wondering just what it means that my score is so low. And falling. I even investigate this Purpose Pact thing to suggest it to clients.

Googling Hawthorne brings me to a frightening article written by a former advisor with the company. Like me, he started his own brokerage under their corporate banner. My teeth now gritted, I read on to learn that by accepting their terms, both of us have unwittingly "also agreed to allow Hawthorne AIs to surveil *all* online activities."

Even scarier, this other broker reported strange account activity once his score began dropping. "Luckily, I managed to turn it around before it fell to one star."

—

Amber makes the turn into Javier's, a Mexican restaurant with a neon mustachioed man in a sombrero on the roof. It's not "authentic" cuisine Bethany has told me more than once—but that's not why Denise picked it.

"I want a place big enough for all your clients to congratulate you," she told me. "This is the beginning of a new chapter in your life."

"Our lives," I reminded her. She liked that.

Scanning the packed parking lot, I can see now she made the right choice. Already, friends crowd the door, some with balloons in hand, others with presents, even though the invitation specifically told them not to bring anything. "We only request your presence today," I instructed Denise to write.

She turns to me and smiles, patting me on the leg.

Gazing into her eyes, I'm transported to the days when Amber was little Spence's age. A smattering of crow's feet frame her eyes, the only real sign I can detect of her age. To me, Denise still looks just as beautiful as she did the week I took off so we could "honeymoon" at our little home in Fort Myers.

"They're all here for you," she tells me happily.

I'm about to respond when my phone buzzes. I wish I could say I felt that absence of fear Davis enjoyed the day he retired. Instead, something gnaws at me. Something not right.

"Excuse me," I say.

I check my phone to see there's an alert waiting with the Hawthorne logo. "After reviewing your accounts, we have determined your personal investing history is in breach of our community guidelines."

"Dad? Are you okay?" Amber asks from the front seat.

I open my email to see Hawthorne has sent me a message. It's a company alert that all my brokerage accounts are under review. Even little Spence's.

"*No.*"

Fear floods my being.

A knock on the car window makes me jump. It's the Melvilles. A couple our age, I began advising them decades ago. "Is this where the party is?" Clyde Melville grins. His wife, Betsy, waves happily.

Sweat forms on my upper lip. My hands shake so badly I can hardly type as I try to pull up the account I set up for little Spence. This morning it held more than $1,000,000 in liquid funds. When I get to the page, it's grayed out just like all my other accounts, preventing me from accessing all that money I stockpiled over the years.

Just then Bethany and her husband pull up beside us. On the side of their van is a paper sign reading, "Next stop: Venice, Italy." Beside it is a picture of Denise and me from our wedding. I look past it to see more friends and clients crowding the parking lot. A terrible old feeling returns: shame.

"Theo?" asks Denise, worry in her voice.

"*Dad?* What's wrong?"

A notification flashes on my phone, alerting me my advisor ranking has dropped to one star. *This can't be happening.* I start to call Hawthorne for an explanation but remember the only way to reach them is through the AI bots.

TELL

If you are of a certain age, you remember Victoria's Secret as the little mall shop selling bras and panties. Women went there to buy cute teddies to spice up the bedroom. Men liked it because it gave them a way to surprise their girlfriend or wife with tasteful yet titillating lingerie.

Then in April 2022, the company did something off-brand: it broadcast its first-ever *male* celebrity model. As part of its new athleisure line intended for the younger set, it brought on actor Darren Barnet to promote gender-free fare, including hoodies and workout apparel.[1]

But *was* this move off-brand? Might it involve something deeper? Determining Victoria's Secret's motivations requires a small historical detour. The acronym ESG is largely meaningless to many people, but it stands for three broad categories of interest for so-called socially responsible investors:

> *Environmental:* pertaining to a company's use of energy sources, especially around climate change. It can also concern waste management and pollution.

Social: often relates to a company's relationship to its staff, including workplace conditions and pay. It can also concern an organization's customer relations, its stated mission, and even its public or political stance on issues.

Governance: how a company is managed or led by the executive team. At stake can be how well the C-suite attends to the concerns of stakeholders, such as the board, shareholders, investors, customers, and workers.

Though ESG isn't (yet) a major topic among the public, it has been around for more than a decade. According to contributor Betsy Atkins, writing for *Forbes*, "ESG issues were first mentioned in the 2006 United Nation's Principles for Responsible Investment (PRI) report consisting of the Freshfield Report and 'Who Cares Wins.' ESG criteria was, for the first time, required to be incorporated in the financial evaluations of companies. This effort was focused on further developing sustainable investments. At the time, 63 investment companies composed of asset owners, asset managers and service providers signed with $6.5 trillion in assets under management (AUM) incorporating ESG issues."[2]

In December 2021, ESG funds under management in the United States were nearly $360 billion, according to SustainFi.[3] That's a breathtaking sum of money. To put it in context, the Institutional Investor reports the full amount of assets under management globally as of 2020 is $103 trillion.[4] This means that a vast amount of the total market value of investments managed by a person or entity now participate in the ESG scheme.

What scheme is that?

Put simply, ESG is a rating that companies receive. It grades them on their ESG compliance. "Environmental, social, and governance (ESG) scores—a social credit framework for sustainability reporting—are being used as the primary mechanism to achieve the shift to a stakeholder model," explains the think tank Heartland. "They measure both financial and non-financial impacts of investments and companies and serve to formally institutionalize corporate social responsibility in global economic infrastructure."[5]

What's wrong with that? you may be wondering. *Isn't it a good thing that businesses are finally graded on their activities? Won't this lead to less pollution and more benevolent corporate cultures?*

Maybe. Or maybe ESG is a cleverly engineered carrot-and-stick tactic to control companies—not unlike how China's social credit system controls people.

At least that's the conclusion Elon Musk reached. On April 2, 2022, he tweeted, "I am increasingly convinced that corporate ESG is the Devil Incarnate."[6]

Now why might the richest man in the world say this? It comes down to *conformity*. Baked into any social credit system—personal or corporate—is the idea one should modify one's behavior to comply with accepted standards or rules.

Virtue signaling is never far behind conformity. It's just more visible now that we are so connected online. It's not enough that we comply with prevailing conventions. In the Twitter age, we must also broadcast to the world our compliance to garner accolades, thereby boosting our social perception.

And it's not just Twitter.

On *every* social media platform, you'll find people quick to show you that they care about others—that they possess integrity. What this really means? They agree with whatever the "hive mind" deems ethical at that moment.

The meme "I support the current thing" went viral in 2022 for capturing just this mindset. As *Know Your Meme* reports, this slogan is "often paired with the NPC Wojak character to mock people on social media who change their profile pictures to include symbols or filters that show support for a particular movement or ideology."[7] (NPC

Wojak refers to a nonplayer character within video games.) Its inclusion in this context is meant to denounce those who do not think for themselves but, rather, take their marching orders from the zeitgeist. The late Soviet Union strongman Vladimir Lenin is reported to have called them "useful idiots"[8] (a derogatory term for mindless people who go along with whatever seems popular or admired); he saw their utility for action once propagandized.

Kim Iversen, former cohost of the *Hill*'s news program *Rising*, equally sees through people (and now companies) professing their integrity to earn points in the public arena. She connected the ESG dots brilliantly on the show in April 2022 by suggesting that such posturing is not about integrity. It's about using our inherent desire for social acceptance to reward some companies while punishing others. In other words, to command obedience.

To illustrate ESG's hollowness, Iversen brought up the fact that centralized gatekeepers are the ones who get to decide the scores of companies, a power with profound implications. She brought up Tesla, a company that makes electric vehicles. According to letter "E" of the sham rubric, Tesla should receive a high grade for its commitment to the environment, right? Wrong. "Tesla . . . has a moderate to a moderately poor score," said Iversen.[9]

How can this be?

The answer is simple. Tesla's low ESG score is not based so much on the automaker's commitment to clean energy. It's due to the powers-that-be's disapproval of its CEO Elon Musk: "The scoring system takes into account his eclectic personality, his tendency to tweet whatever he wants, his views on COVID, and his libertarian politics," said Iversen.[10] (Interesting sidenote: Tesla's score even trails gas-guzzling companies like Ford.)

But it gets more preposterous.

As Iversen reports, the weapons manufacturer Lockheed Martin, known for producing bombs and missiles to rain death from the skies, also has a better social score than Tesla. "Why is that? . . . It's because ESG scores are based on what neoliberal elites consider to be moral and good," said Iversen. "It's *good* to supply weapons to our so-called friends, they use them to kill 'bad guys.' Never mind the fact that they also kill children. But it's *bad* to criticize COVID lockdown policies."[11]

Also, in case you were wondering which company reigns at the apex of the ESG scheme? It's Microsoft Corporation. We'll let you draw your own conclusions.

Armed with this background, let's return to Victoria's Secret and the question we posed earlier: Why might a company known for women's lingerie suddenly promote a male model to represent it? "The move is part of the underwear giant's efforts to rehabilitate its brand, long accused of promoting unattainable beauty standards that cater to the male gaze and that negatively affect young people's self-esteem," explains Tiffany Ap for *Quartz*. "It's nixed its famous televised fashion show, and diversified its model line-up."[12]

We might say it's a *vastly* different brand approach, one driven not so much by appealing to what used to bring men and women to Victoria's Secret stores—lingerie—but rather a cynical effort to virtue signal.

Don't believe us? In 2021, the company produced its first ESG report. CEO Martin Waters accompanied the announcement with a not-so-subtle message for those in the know. "We have launched the next stage of this mission by organizing our efforts around an intentional environmental, social and governance (ESG) structure and starting the very necessary work of embedding diversity, equity and inclusion (DEI) into all facets of our business. We refer to this journey as *Consciously Designing Positive Change*."[13]

In the same announcement, Waters describes how his newly

rebranded organization is complying with the kinds of virtue signaling so necessary to achieve that coveted ESG score. For example, the company:

- Established a new board of directors of which 86 percent were women and 43 percent were racially diverse

- Hired a chief diversity officer and built a DEI strategy

- Committed to continuously reviewing its compensation practices to provide equal pay for equal work for employees across all gender identities and races

- Regularly assessed its suppliers' compliance with its environmental policies, including chemical use and wastewater management

- Increased its use of preferred fibers, including recycled polyester and recycled polyamide, and promised to set specific sustainable product goals in 2022[14]

Whatever happened to making lingerie that people like?

—

The idea that corporations must now go to such lengths to play the game for social acceptance may feel unprecedented and frightening, but it's not so novel. As the saying goes, "There's nothing new under the sun."

In the 1950s, American playwright Arthur Miller penned *The Crucible*. Ostensibly, it's a retelling of the Salem Witch Trials in which a small New England town became swept up in moral panic, leading citizens to try and execute innocent people for the crime of "witchcraft."

Really, it was an allegory about how hive-mind groupthink can poison communities. Back then, Miller was commenting on his fears concerning McCarthyism, but his message is still just as apt. All these years later, the threat of mob rule is alive and well. The difference? Now it's abetted by centralized tyranny involving the richest, most powerful companies on earth.

And if we are not careful, just like Theo, we may soon find ourselves at the mercy of this mob, not just for our livelihoods but for our very way of life.

4

PANOPTICON

SHOW

I run the guy's socials. It's unbelievable. He hasn't had a bad tweet since 2021. But he can't be a saint, either. Otherwise, they wouldn't have hired me. More on that in a minute.

For now, it's up to me to make one Joseph R. Kreuter look bad, optics-wise. That's why I spent my morning mainlining cups of coffee as I combed his Wiki page, his YouTube channel, all his platforms.

He posted typical CEO thought-leader bromides you'd expect from a start-up cowboy spearheading an SaaS company. From his TED Talk:

"Change is inevitable. How you *manage* change is what counts." Obvious.

"Alter your perception, alter your reality." Yeah, right.

"Be the disruption you wish to see in the world." Think he stole that last one from Gandhi. Keep that little fact in my back pocket.

PanOpticon sends me a text. Carrie wants progress. "He's still on the board. WTF?"

Three little dots appear, signaling she's got more to say. Like the furrow of the brow before lips move. Her mind's gears at work. Then they're gone.

Looking up, I see a ticker tape headline scroll across my office TV. *Flight delays due to inclement weather in the northeast. Retail rebounding in Q4 . . .*

I stop myself from blasting Carrie with an angry text. Clients never get the work we do. They don't realize it's not so easy to get someone canceled. Especially squeaky-clean Mr. Kreuter with his backlog of inspirational Insta posts. His every TikTok clips all but scream, "Look at me. I'm normal. *Likable*."

Taking another pull from my Lavazza, I hop to my feet for some carpet pacing. I've been in situations like this before. Mrs. Breyers comes to mind. Real nonstarter of a case. At least at first.

Pic after pic reinforced her image as Mom of the Year. Soccer pick-ups. Etsy-quality family art projects. Tasteful Halloween snaps with the kids. (She opted for wholesomeness rather than dressing like a tart. Noted.)

Same as now, PanOpticon kept screaming in my ear all the while. "*Optics*. Get us something bad or Mr. Breyers will lose his custody battle." Carrie warned me what that would mean in her singsong voice. "She don't get flayed; you don't get paid."

Only never count Sam Spear out when money is on the line.

The breakthrough happened a week later. And not because I resorted to deep fakery like some other agents I know. *Ellis*. Guy would rather spend weeks fusing a mark's lips with implicating dialogue.

Not me. I'm for old-fashioned detective work. Besides, deep fakes can blow up in your face, costing you big dough when it all goes *bang*. Ellis knew that better than anyone. So did his creditors.

But back to hitting pay dirt.

Turned out Spotless Mrs. Breyers did have a spot. All it took was some ingenuity. And a fake CV and a bogus job interview. You see, in addition to being Number-One Mom, Mrs. Breyers led a telehealth company.

The funny part? She still face-to-faces with job applicants. So Mr. Sam Spear became Dr. Theodore Dertzel, licensed addiction specialist. His forte? Getting addicts off opioids without resorting to methadone.

At least that's what my ersatz resume said.

Truth be told, I didn't *not* like Mrs. Breyers when we met in person. Her personal fastidiousness extended to her décor. All straight lines and open space, her tidy office matched her friendly half smile.

But a man's gotta eat.

And I knew just where to stick my knife when she exposed her flank. Like every other self-respecting agent, I had an I-Cam procedure. My eyes and ears afford me high-def video surveillance, including sound capabilities. Better than any London intersection, I'm a walking, talking CCTV intelligencer vacuuming up marks' data. Probing for weaknesses. Exploiting errors *and* omissions.

That's why when pretty Mrs. Breyers with her high-minded ideals espoused her corporate credo, my chest expanded. I could breathe again.

"At BeWellFast," she said, "we don't hire Asians, Whites, Blacks, or Latinos. We also don't hire based on religion. Gays or straights. We hire *talented* people—regardless of skin tone, sexual orientation, or religion."

"You do?" I couldn't believe my luck. Her virtue would be her undoing.

"That's the way every company should view prospects. Potential hires should be based on merit. Experience. Talent. Of course, at BeWellFast we have one more requirement. *Compassion* for others."

The clip went viral.

Within twenty-four hours, not only did Mrs. Breyers have to resign from the company she built, but her Personal Credit Score inverted as well. Instantly locked out of her office building and her co-op, she couldn't even check in at a hotel. At least not a nice one. Her bank also froze her funds for internal review.

"Mrs. Breyers' words do not represent BeWellFast culture," John Knowles, the company's transitional CEO tweeted before the day ended. "Tone-deaf and insensitive, they don't reflect our anti-hate values."

Every social media outlet piled on Mrs. Breyers, accusing her of breathtaking villainy—especially when she made the mistake of doubling down on her desire to be nondiscriminatory in her hiring decisions.

As you might guess, the family law judge granted Mr. Breyers full custody soon after. Before court adjourned, Pan0pticon's ACH hit my account.

But I can't rest on my laurels. Or expect Mr. Kreuter's takedown to be as easy. Besides, he must have pissed off someone bad. My daily alone for this job exceeds what I brought in last quarter. And the client agreed to cover expenses.

But only if I pull this off.

Buzz. Another text from Carrie: "Client just gave word they're pulling the contract unless it's done by noon."

I check the time. *Shit.* That's less than three hours.

"But—" I start to write and then think better of it.

Clock's ticking. Best be on my way.

—

I wish I could say I had a plan to incriminate my mark when I began trailing him in West Hollywood, but I didn't. Out of ideas and time,

I needed to stage an incident on the fly. To improvise. It was my last chance.

Mr. Kreuter's gait doesn't scream Master of the Universe despite his $10,000 sports jacket and designer jeans. He bobs and weaves like the other ARglassed denizens strolling Melrose, half in this reality, half in the 'Verse.

He halts to tie his shoe. Or at least that's what I think he's doing until I get a better look. Crouched on the sidewalk, he's fully immersed—in watching a line of ants carry a big dead spider above their heads.

I've seen marks do weird things like this before. It's easy to get caught up in an interesting ARglasses data scroll. A thumbnail vid probably just appeared in Kreuter's periph. Most likely some E. O. Wilson doc explaining how the insects' pheromones help lead hunting parties back to their colony.

I flash to a sunny beach in my mind. Remembering how my little son Scotty and I once spent a whole afternoon digging holes for ants. That was years ago, before my own custody battle.

I do a double take. The spider isn't dead after all. He makes a move to escape the ants' clutches. It works. For a second.

But there are too many of them. Working feverishly, a mob of thin little arms and legs capture him again, carting the spider off to the grass. God knows what'll happen to him.

Kreuter continues, and so do I. I follow him into an apparel boutique. A handful of customers serve here as helpful camouflage. They allow me to blend in among the racks of trendy clothes.

Not that Kreuter is on to me in the slightest. Straddling multiple realities like so many other customers, he uses his ARglasses to gain intel on garments.

"Can I help you, sir?" I hear a man behind me say.

Damn. Now I'm going to have to pretend to be a customer too.

"Um, yeah." I turn to see a heavyset clerk with a neck tattoo, spiky green hair, and those huge earrings that stretch your earlobes. "Looking for pants."

"Perfect. My name is Clyde. Right this way."

Clyde leads me to the other side, waddling as he goes, he's so obese.

"Here you are. Just let me know if you need the fitting room."

"Thanks."

Inwardly I curse him for taking me away from Kreuter. For ten minutes I pretend to browse pants just so I can keep watch on my guy. Nothing happens. He just goes from rack to rack, checking clothing specs on his ARglasses.

Meanwhile, I'm burning daylight. In twenty-six minutes, this job is gone. And so's my money.

Buzz. Another text from Carrie: "BTW, you're gonna owe us the per diem we fronted you." Next to it are three cash emojis and a mad face.

I sigh. That's a lot of money to pay back. Funds I don't have.

Out of ideas, I wander over to Kreuter, overhearing him ask a different clerk for fitting room access. Given a key fob, he goes in to try on some jackets.

I check my phone again. Fourteen minutes left.

I happen to look up and see the immense vision of Clyde outside Kreuter's fitting room.

He knocks on the door. "Yoo-hoo. Anyone in there?"

The second Kreuter opens the door, my problems vanish into thin air.

I caught it. Someone else—*a rookie*—might've missed it. Not me. There's a reason I set my I-Cam to capture micro-expressions, those nearly imperceptible "tells" our faces betray. They reveal our real thoughts, our real emotions.

And what did Mr. Kreuter's show? Fat people like Clyde gross him out.

His disgust registered for only a nanosecond, but it was more than enough. I engage the SmartEdit on my phone after downloading the shot. Combining slow-mo to the closeup will blow out this scene so it looks like Kreuter's disgust occurred for longer than it did—and appears way worse.

Within hours the whole world will know that Kreuter hates fat people. *Bye-bye, SaaS company. Bye-bye, thought leadership*. I'll even bet TED pulls his talk.

Turning to go, I begin composing my congratulatory text to Carrie.

"So long now," I hear Clyde say behind me.

I don't look back.

—

Squeezing into a booth at a nearby coffee shop, I check the time. Three minutes to go. My SmartEdit alert tells me my video is ready. I pull up the video and gasp.

There must be some mistake. It shows a video of those ants carrying the big spider on their spindly backs.

"What the—?"

"It's gone."

Clyde sits down beside me. Except this is a thinner version. Without dramatic earrings, spiky hair, and former girth, he looks like . . .

"*Ellis?*"

"In the flesh," he winks. "Only less of it."

My colleague. The same hack who uses deep fakes to take down marks.

"W-what are you doing here?"

Ellis hands me a business card. "Working for ReputatiOn."

It feels like someone just put my rib cage in a vise. I can't breathe.

"Kreuter hired you?"

"By way of Pan0pticon. Same company. Different departments. It's a new thing."

"And you hacked my SmartEdit?"

"You're not the only agent who stalks his marks." Ellis throws his fat suit on the table. "This was just to buy me time. Looks like your contract ran out."

I look at the clock on my phone. It reads 12:00 p.m. Beneath it, the video plays the clip of dozens of ants carrying off their prey.

TELL

In 2016, Netflix's *Black Mirror* aired a now infamous episode titled "Nosedive." Shot with beautiful high-key lighting, it offered a horrific vision. A young woman named Lacie Pound lives in a not-so-distant future where anyone can rate your social profile based on what you say and do.[1]

Like most everyone in this story, Lacie strives to be well perceived online. Only her popularity bid has major real-world ramifications. At the beginning, she has an approval rating of 4.2 out of 5. Considered to be an average score, it hurts her chances to live in a better housing estate or even obtain a good seat on a flight.

Lacie sees her chance to improve her societal standing when her old friend Naomi (with a 4.8 rating) asks her to be her maid of honor. Naomi and her upper-class friends (those with ratings of 4.5 or higher) enjoy a privileged life of ease and comfort because of their strong scores. If only Lacie can nail a great wedding speech, she, too, could enjoy the good life.

Or so she thinks.

Instead, a series of misfortunes and misunderstandings decimate Lacie's score, destroying her life. In a related fashion, anyone who has ever had a business knows how such a seemingly innocuous rating scheme can maim your reputation. Imagine you own a restaurant. Someone could claim they got food poisoning at your place and post a bad review on Yelp. It doesn't matter if it's true or not; the damage will be done. Until such time as the review disappears—something that's unlikely to happen—anyone who visits your page can see it and is likely to believe the accusation.

Former 49ers quarterback Steve Young is commonly quoted as saying the reason why: "Perception is reality. If you are perceived to be something, you might as well be it because that's the truth in people's minds." This is especially evident when it comes to how social media helps us make snap decisions about others.

Decades before Facebook was a glint in CEO Mark Zuckerberg's eye, Daniel J. Boorstin wrote *The Image: A Guide to Pseudo-events in America*. Published in 1962, it predicted the twenty-first-century milieu, an era where staged press conferences outshine actual news events—a zeitgeist in which an influencer can become a celebrity as a "person who is known for his well-knownness." As Boorstin writes, "We have become so accustomed to our illusions that we mistake them for reality."[2]

But the horrors of an episode like "Nosedive" aren't the stuff of fiction. Perceptions rule reality. And they are currently being exploited to savage ends through China's social credit system. The People's Republic of China now uses extreme surveillance to control its population via technocratic centralization that yesterday's most ambitious despots could scarcely imagine.

As Katie Canales explained for *Business Insider* in 2021, "Like private credit scores, a person's social score can move up and down depending on their behavior. The exact methodology is a secret—but examples of infractions include bad driving, smoking in nonsmoking zones, buying too many video games, and posting fake news online, specifically about terrorist attacks or airport security."[3]

Punishments for those with low social credit scores align with "Nosedive" in a perverse example of life imitating art. For instance, China restricts "bad" people from traveling. In 2018, the government prevented citizens from buying flights nearly 20 million times.

That's not all. Today, the many Lacies of China can also expect to be banned or restricted from accessing the following:

- Hotels
- Housing
- Medical checkups and/or procedures
- Job opportunities
- Banking activities

Instead, they are blacklisted based on data obtained and submitted to authorities and held in the National Credit Information Sharing Platform, a centralized database. Much like ESG ratings, businesses are also subject to the same surveillance and ranking and can be "blacklisted" for condemned activities. As *China Briefing* explains:

> China's social credit system is an ambitious initiative to build a database that monitors individual, corporate, and government behavior across the country in real time. According to the Chinese government, the system will use big data to build a high-trust society where individuals and organizations follow the law. It will do so by assigning social credit scores to each entity based on their behavior, which are translated into a variety of rewards and punishments.[4]

Of course, none of this centralized control would be possible a few years ago before smartphones, AI, and tech-enabled panopticon-style surveillance. For those unfamiliar with the latter term, it originated in the eighteenth century. At the time, philosopher Jeremy Bentham conceived of a panopticon as a cutting-edge prison. "It consisted of a circular, glass-roofed, tanklike structure with cells along the external wall facing toward a central rotunda; guards stationed in the rotunda could keep all the inmates in the surrounding cells under constant surveillance," according to *Britannica*.[5]

It's interesting to note that Bentham is also regarded as the founder of utilitarianism, a "theory of morality that advocates actions that foster happiness or pleasure and oppose actions that cause unhappiness or harm," as *Investopedia* explains.[6] The basic idea is that individuals and groups should pursue activities that produce the greater benefit for the largest number of people.

Like the social credit system or the panopticon, this ethos might seem good—in theory. In practice, it's a nightmare.

It doesn't take much to realize that utilitarianism could lead to all kinds of atrocities in the name of collectivism. Here's one example. What if the leader of a nation decreed slavery to be legal as long as a tiny number of slaves toiled for the greater number of citizens? Employing utilitarianist ethics, this could be deemed okay. What's so bad about the suffering of a half-dozen slaves compared to the profound happiness of a million citizens? The latter could enjoy comfortable lives on the backs of an inconsequential number of slaves. Even better, should the state decide that these slaves had committed despicable crimes, their offenses would more than justify their punishment.

But we could go one step further.

Eager to pursue activities that produce the greater benefit for the largest number of people, our great leader, in his or her infinite wisdom, might also determine that these criminals' wrongs were so abhorrent, the masses would benefit from watching them fight to death *Hunger Games*–style.

Not only would such carnage provide the people with a form of amusement, but it could also lead to strong ticket sales, itself a boon for the economy. But why stop there? Why not invent new forms of torture for our criminal slaves? Some die-hard fans might even pay more for the chance to watch the cruelty in private VIP rooms, again benefitting the economy.

Though exaggerated in its depravity, this scenario demonstrates what happens when we combine a collectivist mentality with a centralization of power. It also foreshadows great suffering to come should we encourage *outrage culture* where the perceptions of others may be manipulated to satiate society's basest desires.

Consider the Sixth Amendment of the U.S. Constitution, which reads as follows:

> In all criminal prosecutions, the accused shall enjoy the right to a speedy and public trial, by an impartial jury of the State and district wherein the crime shall have been committed, which district shall have been previously ascertained by law, and to be informed of the nature and cause of the accusation; to be confronted with the witnesses against him; to have compulsory process for obtaining witnesses in his favor, and to have the Assistance of Counsel for his defense.[7]

Prescient as they were, our Founding Fathers couldn't imagine a day in which the court of public opinion could try *and* convict the accused in the brief span it takes to watch a video of a job interview or a person coming out of a dressing room. Fantastical as the above neo-noir's premise might strike our current sensibilities, it's not far from happening in real life. Especially should the status quo continue.

Already, China is using such panopticon surveillance tactics on its people. Controlling them. Punishing them. And still the world spins. We like to think we are so free and enlightened in the West. But might we already have created our own version of the techno-panopticon? And how much worse might things get before "We the People" awaken to the growing centralization danger?

5

INSIGHTS

SHOW

"This will go on your permanent record," Mr. Rabe tells Dylan Canfield, the seventeen-year-old junior sitting across from him in English Studies.

No response from Dylan. Unless you count the nearly imperceptible shrug Mr. Rabe sees so many of his students do.

It's five minutes past the fourth-period bell, signaling lunch. Instead of enjoying the falafel wrapped in foil that Cheryl handed him as he hurried out the door, Mr. Rabe sits alone, across from his student.

Beyond their desks, he spies Dylan's classmates scurrying off to the cafeteria. It's May now in Salt Lake City, and the sun shines beautifully, heralding summer, Mr. Rabe's favorite time of year. Yesterday he finalized his list: the dozen books he'll devour in the lazy months ahead.

Mr. Rabe looks the young man over.

Doing so, he plays the game he so often does, trying to see himself in his student when he was his age. Looks-wise, Dylan has him beat. Even though he stupidly wears his hair like the other boys—mostly in his face so you can barely see his eyes—it's clear that Dylan will have no trouble in the romance department.

Although that doesn't seem to interest Dylan. Ever since relocating to this school halfway through the year, he has avoided his peers. Never once has he raised his hand in class.

If it weren't for iNsights, Mr. Rabe would have no clue that Dylan also blows him out of the water in the smarts department. Not just the teen version of himself, either. The assessments on Dylan from his last school show the young man isn't only college-level competent. He's brilliant enough to be teaching the courses, if not writing the textbooks.

"I'm not saying this to come down on you," Mr. Rabe tries again. Inwardly cringing, at forty-five he reminds himself of all those nagging teachers that once annoyed him and his friends. "But this is serious. You must apply yourself more."

"Got it." Dylan looks up, firing off words like bullets. "Can I go now?"

"Not yet," says Mr. Rabe, trying to keep it light.

"Why am I even here? I haven't cheated on my assignments."

"I know that. You don't have to."

"I don't mess with anybody."

"I know that too." Mr. Rabe softens his reprimand with a smile. "You haven't *talked* to any of your classmates since you got here."

Dylan kicks his long legs out, folding his arms back. "Look. My headset said I read that book I was supposed to. I finished it."

"I know you did. And how'd you feel about *Lord of the Flies*?"

"Fine."

"*Lord of the Flies* was fine?"

Dylan stares out the window. It's clear he wishes this conversation would end. Again, Mr. Rabe casts himself back to his high school days. While he was no teacher's pet or budding scholar, he connected with books. English was the subject that excited him most. He loved discussing ideas in class.

"Don't you have any other feedback? Anything you can share with me if you won't talk in class?"

No response.

"Were you surprised by how the boys turned on each other? How they killed Piggy?"

"Uh-huh." Dylan might have been agreeing with him on the weather.

Mr. Rabe rises from his chair.

Like all the classrooms in Davenport Unified, his comes equipped with the latest AR monitor. Using hologram tech, it presents a three-dimensional touch screen (except without the need to touch anything). The moment his fingers "touch" the air containing an image, he's taken to a different application, not unlike a phone.

Trying another tactic, Mr. Rabe pulls up iNsights, the district's educational backbone. On-screen, he plays back a video. Taken last week, it shows Dylan's face and the text of William Golding's novel side by side. The recording occurred at home while Dylan read his assignment hooked up to an eduheadset resembling an oculus. As with all students at Davenport, his device monitored his cognition and biometric responses as he read along.

Pulling his two fingers apart on the hologram, Mr. Rabe expands the image on-screen. "This shows me not only where you lost interest—page forty-seven—but the exact word where your concentration wandered. It was *the*, in case you're wondering."

"Uh-huh."

Mr. Rabe walks away from the monitor. Laying his hands on his desk, leaning forward, he finds himself in a not unfamiliar experience: imposter syndrome. *What am I doing here? Am I just a fraud?* Looking past a framed photo of himself and Cheryl vacationing in Sicily, he imagines himself in any number of feel-good teacher movies. *Stand and Deliver . . . Lean on Me . . .*

Only he's not fooling himself.

Well-meaning and well-behaved, his students are nothing like the juvenile delinquents in those storylines. And if he's being honest, he's no transformational lightning-in-a-bottle educationist. He's a middling middle-aged teacher who'd rather be cozied up with a Howard Zinn hardcover and a steaming cup of chamomile.

When Mr. Rabe looks back at Dylan, he sees the young man has his phone out, typing away with two thumbs. "Can I go now?"

Mr. Rabe looks at the clock.

If they end the discussion here, he could still enjoy a good thirty minutes of reading in the teacher's lounge. Plus, that falafel is calling him.

No. That's the easy way out.

Mr. Rabe slides back into his chair. "You know that eduheadset tracks your eye movements as you read assignments? It does that so teachers like me can better measure the kinds of educational content you might respond to."

Dylan doesn't bother to put down his phone. "So I've been told."

"But you're also intelligent enough to know there's another reason for all the data gathering we do at this school."

For a second Mr. Rabe is hopeful this compliment might appeal to Dylan's vanity. No dice. He stays nonresponsive.

"All that biometric data we collect tells us the academic story about *you*, Dylan. Using data points like micro expressions, galvanic skin response, even eye dilation, we can tell your feelings. How enthusiastic you are about what you're learning. Did you know that?"

The blank look coming from Dylan cuts worse than any sarcastic eye roll. It's more painful than being talked back to—something Mr. Rabe hasn't experienced since his early teaching days. Dylan's expression reveals that not only does he know all this, but he also doesn't give a flying f—.

"Now that I know your feelings about reading and this book, it's my job to *change* those feelings. To get you back on track."

Dylan has gone icy cold.

It's clear that he sees past Mr. Rabe's feeble attempt at being the teacher with heart. The idea of escaping to the teacher's lounge seems better than ever. *Let it go. A few more weeks and the semester is over. School is over.*

Mr. Rabe might yield to that siren song if not for the lame poster behind Dylan. Staring past the young man, his gaze lands on Winston Churchill. Beneath a black-and-white photo of the statesman is the famous line, "If you're going through hell, keep going."

Damn him.

He never liked Churchill and doubts the man ever said that. What stops Mr. Rabe from abandoning this whole ordeal is the memory of Cheryl helping him put the poster up.

That was ten years ago. Back then, it was the *two* of them in this fight.

"You know, college might seem far off now," Mr. Rabe tells Dylan. "But I promise it'll be here in a blink of an eye. You know where you're going?"

"Not going."

Mr. Rabe nearly falls out of his chair. "Why not? A young man of your capabilities and you don't want to go to college? What'll you do with yourself?"

Dylan shrugs again.

Something snaps in Mr. Rabe. He starts pacing the room so fast he must push his brown tie back to the front when it flies past his shoulder. It occurs to him he's going about this wrong. He has to stop being the educator who has it all together. He must go at this with Brené Brown–esque vulnerability.

"Dylan, I want to tell you something personal. My dream as a young man was to solve mysteries. I grew up reading crime authors like Agatha Christie."

Mr. Rabe turns to see that Dylan is listening.

Emboldened, he continues. "In the early days of the internet, there were these documentary sites about conspiracies. One of them was about the Great Pyramid in Egypt. There're all these weird anomalies. For one thing, the pyramid was made from an estimated 2.3 million blocks of limestone. How did slaves lug all that, much less construct a pyramid of perfect proportions?"

Dylan doesn't respond, but he doesn't look away, either.

Mr. Rabe keeps going. "Here's something else. Did you know it's located precisely on the thirtieth degree, halfway between the equator and the north pole? That means it's locked into the planet's true cardinal directions: north, south, east, and west. Even weirder? If you multiply the Great Pyramid's base perimeter (3,024 feet) by 43,200, you get Earth's equatorial circumference. And if you multiply its height (481 feet) by 43,200, you're left with Earth's polar radius. Isn't that nuts?"

Dylan nods at that. "Yeah."

Mr. Rabe is on a roll. "Strangest of all, the three pyramids of Giza are an exact reproduction of the three stars in Orion's Belt: Delta Orionis (Mintaka), Epsilon (Alnilam), and Zeta (Alnitak). Now, how did these supposedly 'primitive' people living thousands of years ago have the know-how and technology to pull off something this head-scratching?"

"I don't know."

Mr. Rabe flops back into his chair. "Me neither. That's why I wanted to be an archaeologist. To figure out this mystery."

"So why didn't you?"

Encouraged, Mr. Rabe is tempted to tell him the truth, how his graduate degrees saddled him with too much debt to afford his dream, but he stops himself. This is his attempt to get Dylan to try harder, to rethink college—he'd better not undermine it with cold, hard reality.

"Life happens. The important thing here was my dream. I wanted to solve mysteries. That led me to be a teacher, actually. These days my *students* are my mysteries. My job is to solve what it is that makes them tick."

Mr. Rabe had hoped this speech—honestly, his best to date—might move the needle with Dylan. No such luck. The young man clams right up again.

"Don't you have any mysteries you want to solve?"

Dylan goes back to his usual shrugging.

But Mr. Rabe isn't hopeless. Dylan's reticence fuels him. It also convinces him to try another approach. "I have a hunch about something."

Returning to the AR vidscreen, Mr. Rabe punches up iNsights Math. He remembers seeing impressive scores from Dylan's last high school.

"What's the square root of 18,075?" Mr. Rabe asks, feeling foolish himself for not knowing what a square root is, much less the answer.

"134.443296597," says Dylan without hesitation.

"Correct," says iNsights AI, the machine learning algorithm monitoring all classrooms, not unlike Alexa in Dylan's own house.

Impressed, Mr. Rabe presses his case. As soon as he says, "iNsights World Geography," a blank world map appears on-screen.

"I want you to label each country where it belongs," says Mr. Rabe.

"Do I have to? Look, lunch is almost over—"

"You're not leaving this room until you do."

"But this isn't even math or geography class. Why do I have to do this?"

"This is your future!"

Slowly, and exhibiting all the annoyance of youth toward one's elders, Dylan approaches the virtual board. Beginning with Germany and ending with Poland, Dylan correctly labels each country. He then completes Africa and Asia, though he wasn't asked to include them. Each entry is 100 percent correct.

Floored, Mr. Rabe hides his admiration. "Now their capitals."

Dylan lists these perfectly too.

"My God, you could do anything you want with that intelligence."

Dylan isn't looking at him anymore. He's gone back to his phone.

"What do you want to do with all that smarts?"

No response.

"Dylan?"

"I said, what do you want to do with all your brilliance?"

Dylan shrugs. "Video games?"

—

That night Mr. Rabe lies in bed, agitated. Lacking children of their own, he and Cheryl threw themselves into education years ago. The more ambitious of the two, his wife rose through the ranks, becoming principal of a high school in a neighboring county. It was the last educator position she ever held.

"You promised not to bring problems home." Cheryl rolls over in bed to meet his eye.

"I know, I know. But this one's different."

She grins, letting the frustration ebb from her voice as she pets their fat tabby named Sandy. Their cat likes Cheryl best and often steals her pillow in the middle of the night. "That's what you always say, Jim."

"No, I mean it. This young man's assessments are off the charts."

As soon as she hears the word *assessments*, Cheryl is up so fast that she spooks Sandy, sending her out the door. A tall, sinewy woman, Cheryl rises to her full height. Whenever they have these conversations, she falls into her habit of cleaning as a defense mechanism. Already, she's found the dusting spray. Using a damp cloth, she goes to work on their windowsills.

Mr. Rabe sees that they don't need her handiwork, but Cheryl does her routine all the same. "Can you stop that? I'm trying to talk."

She won't stop. "You know my feelings on those assessments."

"Forget about the assessments. I'm talking about a young man's future."

"Don't you see they're one and the same?"

Mr. Rabe sits up in bed. He wears his old striped pajamas that have shrunk from too many washes. The bottom cuffs ride up past his ankles, exposing blond leg hair. "We've had this conversation before—"

"And it never seems to get through that thick skull of yours. That *handsome* thick skull of yours," she adds to show she isn't really mad. "Besides, doesn't all that tinkering and data mining ever bother you?"

"Not like it does you."

"Because I know what it's breeding!"

"*What?* Robots? We're gonna have a nation of robots?"

At that, Mr. Rabe leaps off the bed, impersonating an automaton with stiff, exaggerated arm movements. Cheryl can't help but giggle.

But her levity doesn't last. "It's breeding little rats in cages. Here's some cheese, kids. If you read this book, if you do this assignment—you get your little reward. Today's an A. Tomorrow's college. Yay!"

Mr. Rabe stays calm. "Is that former Principal Rabe talking or Cheryl?"

Her eyes narrow. "You know why I left."

"Yeah, yeah. I've heard it all before. Remote teaching is destroying the classroom experience. Yada yada yada."

Cheryl points her spray bottle at him. "Careful there, Mr. Rabe. I might douse you with this. Besides, that was only *one* part of why I left. It's also because I can't stand all this spying on our kids. It's terrible."

Mr. Rabe takes her hand, bringing her to the foot of the bed, where he sits down. She resists. "I need to clean this."

"No, you don't. It wasn't dirty before you started, and you know it."

Sighing, she allows herself to be dragged over to sit next to him. "I'm serious, Jim. Your heart's in the right place, but whatever you're doing, it's not working. Not because you're a bad teacher. You're one of the best. But you're failing because . . . you're set up to fail."

Mr. Rabe gets up. "I don't believe this."

She pulls him back down. "Your insight thingy, whatever it's called—"

"iNsights."

"Right. iNsights. It works by measuring all this data about your students. Not just their test scores and reading comprehension. Now it's surveilling the kids *themselves*. It's monitoring their internal responses to the curriculum—"

"Yes, so it can be more effective."

"More effective at what? Creating anxiety? Complacency? These kids are told who they are by algorithms before they ever discover anything for themselves."

"Think about Netflix or Amazon. Aren't you glad when it recommends books for you based on your reading history?"

"A little bit," she says with a sigh. "But whatever happened to curiosity? I shudder to think what'll occur when these kids grow up and realize they don't know how to think for themselves. That some big computer in the cloud has been nudging them all their lives into making the 'correct' decision."

Mr. Rabe says nothing. Cheryl leaves the room.

"Where are you going?"

A moment later she returns with a tattered old book. Just seeing its dog-eared pages stirs something within Mr. Rabe. It brings him back to a time thirty years prior, when he was just Jim and summers weren't a paid reprieve from work but, rather, an endless exploration of life's possibilities.

Opening to the last page, she reads these lines:

> So in America when the sun goes down and I sit on the old broken-down river pier watching the long, long skies over New Jersey and sense all that raw land that rolls in one unbelievable huge bulge over to the West Coast, and all that road going, all the people dreaming in the immensity of it, and in Iowa I know by now the children must be crying in the land where they let the children cry, and tonight the stars'll be out, and don't you know that God is Pooh Bear?[1]

She softly closes his copy of *On the Road*, the novel by Jack Kerouac that kept him spellbound the summer he turned fifteen. Hearing those words, his mind races back to his childhood in Memphis, how those evocative lines lit up the dark corners of his existence, opening him to possibilities and a transcendence that all the ensuing years he lived could scarcely hint at.

"Remember when you read a book like that just to read it?" she asks. "Back then you weren't doing it for credit. Or for some pat on the head. You might read a chapter and then lie back, contemplating it for minutes. Hours. Your mind exploding with thoughts and ideas. How did it make you feel?"

Rather than answer her, Mr. Rabe recounts a different *On the Road* passage from memory:

> The only people for me are the mad ones, the ones who are mad to live, mad to talk, mad to be saved, desirous of everything at the same time, the ones who never yawn or say a commonplace thing, but burn, burn, burn like fabulous yellow roman candles exploding like spiders across the stars and in the middle you see the blue centerlight pop and everybody goes "Awww!"[2]

"It made me feel alive," Mr. Rabe tells Cheryl. "Reading stuff like that gave me a zest for life."

Cheryl sits down beside him. As she does, Sandy hops on her lap. "I don't know what your student's problem is; nor do I know what you're trying to do to make it better. But I do know this. If there's some way you can return that spark to him that you just described, it may help him."

—

Mr. Rabe doesn't sleep much that night.

He lies in bed rereading *On the Road*, making little notes to himself. So far, he had come at the Dylan conundrum from different angles. He began by trying to get the young man to understand the problem's seriousness: how if he didn't apply himself more, he might not get accepted into a good college. When that didn't work, he had appealed to what might be Dylan's vanity about his intelligence. That didn't help, either. Then he had tried describing his own life, thinking that might encourage Dylan, but this also led nowhere. And last, he sought to challenge the young man, to no avail.

Cheryl had offered a different approach.

The more he contemplated it, the more obvious it seemed. *Inspiration* was the ticket. All those teaching movies came back to him. In each, the teacher had motivated his or her students with the most powerful tool in the arsenal: the power of imagination, the power of creativity.

Best of all at this was Robin Williams in *Dead Poets Society*.

Mr. Rabe thinks to himself that if he could somehow summon a modicum of his appeal to greatness, he might break through to Dylan. He could help him see all the potential he possessed. Tapping into his own encouragement abilities, Mr. Rabe could make him see that even if Dylan didn't want to go to college, the sky was his limit. He could be anything he chose; all it took was belief in himself and the same zest for life he once felt.

Stepping out the door the following day, Mr. Rabe feels like a new man. He's on fire as he takes his falafel wrapped in foil from Cheryl.

"You look different today," she comments.

"I *feel* different today." He kisses her on the lips before rushing off.

Eschewing the typical podcasts he usually listens to on his morning commute, Mr. Rabe blasts classic rock he jammed to when he was fifteen. Visions of inspiring Dylan with soaring rhetoric bounce around his brain as he rockets through his morning classes. He can't wait to see the young man.

When fourth period finally rolls around, Mr. Rabe sees Dylan take his seat. As usual, he says nothing to anyone the whole period. Undaunted, Mr. Rabe doesn't press him. Nor does he mention their last conversation.

But right after the bell rings, Mr. Rabe stops him at the door. "Can I have a few more minutes of your time?"

Dylan watches all the other students who are free to go. "*Again?*"

"Yes, please. It won't take long."

Once they're alone, Mr. Rabe launches into his most soaring talking points. He tells the story of his literary heroes growing up, how Kerouac led him to adore other beat authors like Lawrence Ferlinghetti and Allen Ginsberg. How their passion for language encouraged him to read more classics, instilling in him an insatiable curiosity for life and culture, to discern why people act the way they do, and, ultimately, to seek out life's mysteries.

That's when he presents his own dog-eared copy of *On the Road* to Dylan. "This is for you," he says, taking a deep breath. "Think of it as the first chapter of the rest of your life."

Dylan holds the book at arm's length as if it were a piece of stinky cheese.

Mr. Rabe waits for him to say something. Anything.

"I'll try harder," he squeaks at last, his face as dead as ever.

"That's it?"

"Isn't that what you want me to do?"

Defeated, Mr. Rabe sinks into his chair. "Yes. That's what I want you to do."

TELL

"Imagine classrooms outfitted with cameras that run constantly, capturing each child's every facial expression, fidget, and social interaction, every day, all year long. Then imagine on the ceilings of those rooms infrared cameras, documenting the objects that every student touches throughout the day, and microphones, recording every word that each person utters. Picture now the children themselves wearing Fitbit-like devices that track everything from their heart rates to their time between meals. For about a quarter of the day, the students use Chromebooks and learning software that track their every click and keystroke."[3]

This isn't the hysterical ravings of some dystopian sci-fi novel. It comes out of an article from contributing writer Benjamin Herold for *Education Week*. Back in 2016, he trumpeted the vision of one Max Ventilla, CEO of something called AltSchool, a Bay Area start-up using big data analytics to produce "better educational outcomes." In 2019, AltSchool ceased operations, rebranding as a software company called Altitude Learning.

But that doesn't mean the dream of seizing big data capabilities for schooling hasn't died. If anything, it's going stronger than ever, benefitting from widespread remote instruction during the COVID-19 pandemic. More on that in a moment.

For now, it's important to note public schools are amassing vast amounts of information about their students. According to IAPP, the world's largest global information privacy community, "In addition to grades and attendance records, schools often collect everything from a child's 'race and gender to their economic status, behavioral issues, biometric data, health status' and such data is then stored by schools, state databases and other third parties. Potential risks to the students include a breach of their sensitive data, sale of it to third party advertisers or eventual eligibility issues with insurance companies and employers."[4]

Likewise, national research consultant Iris Garner recently broke down the rationale for such vast educational data collection for the company Learning A–Z. "Think of educational data as a machine that receives and uses inputs to help run the educational process, producing outputs that include things like progress, success, and achievement. Data use depends on critical inputs from the parent, teacher, student, district, and state. Specific data inputs can include everything from teacher quality to student demographics, while specific data outputs include things like attendance, grades, assessment scores, and graduation rates."[5]

According to Garner, effective data usage can lead to benefits for students and teachers alike. Districts can use the information from assessments to determine which pupils require additional instruction in which subjects. It's even possible to use such data to "personalize" teaching.[6] As we know, each child learns differently; using AI, in conjunction with vast data streams, it's theoretically possible to pinpoint the best means of teaching students based on their own limitations and abilities.

On its face, this rationale sounds all well and good. But as we have seen so many times in this book, the best-laid intentions can lead to bad outcomes. Hundreds of data points already exist for the average elementary school pupil, telling the story of their successes and failures. This is because as far back as preschool, well-meaning educators sought to measure their progress in various areas, such as reading comprehension, vocabulary, social competence, math skills, and so on.

Of course, school districts compiled this information on students going back decades. The difference is that they can do this now *at scale*, compiling, storing, and interpreting vast amounts of intel no human could possibly manage. Two factors account for these advancements: the falling cost of data storage and rising computing power. It's now possible to granularly track the performance of each student, assessing their strengths and their weaknesses.

Despite so much rhetoric celebrating "the personalization of education," technological advances threaten to undermine our understanding of what it means to be human. Are our kids made to be poked and prodded like cattle before FDA inspectors, immutably relegated to certain stations in life?

This is but one of the many concerns technological centralization poses for the educational sector. Not only does it discount the potential for human growth, but it also conditions young people to view themselves as little more than products in an assembly line. Dare step out from the crowd to your detriment: "This will go (and stay) on your permanent record."

None other than the influential psychologist and father of behavioralist psychology, B. F. Skinner, understood this well. In 2019, Harvard professor Shoshana Zuboff published *The Age of Surveillance Capitalism*, exposing the many ways tech giants like Facebook, Amazon, and most of all Google benefit from spying on customers, using collected data to profit in various ways, but especially via predictive futures. Importantly, Zuboff zeroes in on Skinner's influence on this business model, and its long-term societal dangers.[7]

Throughout her exposé, Zuboff returns to the seemingly innocuous video game craze *Pokémon GO*, so popular with young people Dylan's age in the mid-2010s. According to Zuboff, this phenomenon was little more than a trial balloon, showing Big Tech the power they wield to addict youngsters to a fun pursuit (collecting video sprites in public spaces and even people's yards) while in actuality data mining them.

"The efficacy of Pokémon Go in impelling and directing human behaviour recalls nothing so strongly as the psychologist BF Skinner's development of operant conditioning, and Skinner is one of many figures Zuboff evokes, implicates and critiques in her narrative," writes James Bridle for the *Guardian*. "Skinner developed and perfected a technology of behaviour modification in living organisms, and extrapolated from it a politics rooted in total social control. Published in 1971, his incendiary treatise *Beyond Freedom and Dignity* prescribed a future of behavioural modification and redirection which rejected the very idea of freedom, replacing it with guaranteed outcomes and individual conformity."[8]

For those who don't know, Skinner was vehemently against people obtaining or enjoying freedom. He feared what would happen if individuals woke up to their own power. His books, including *Walden Two* (1948), were arguments for behavior modification technology to control the populace. It just took Silicon Valley a few decades to put his ideas on things like operant conditioning into practice at scale. Nowadays, so many teens who use social media and other technology serve as rats in an endless, nightmarish experiment. Surveilled and nudged, they're pushed toward those behaviors most benefitting their masters' designs.

But there's something even more insidious at play here.

In 2020, best-selling author and futurist Yuval Harari opined the following for *Al Jazeera*: "We are at a watershed moment where surveillance is no longer limited to what we do, but how we feel."[9]

This is critical to understanding the threats we face under technological centralization. Most people can wrap their heads around external reconnaissance—for instance, CCTV camera video recording their every movement. They may also understand how social media companies profile their activities, spying on the photos and updates they post.

But do they understand what's coming next?

Again, according to tech insider Harari, COVID-19 opened the door for governments and other invested entities to surveil people internally.[10] In other words, they could obtain data on what's going on inside our bodies, including our white blood cell count, our blood sugar level, and even our body fat percentage. Of course, the rationale for such intrusion will always be couched in the greater good; in this case, the rationale is public health and safety. Fair enough.

But even if you buy into the need for such extensive investigations of your person, Harari is quick to point out in the same 2020 feature that those doing the spying stand to benefit in other ways. He offers an example that's so dystopian it appears more sci-fi than reality-based: how reading an article or watching the accompanying video could indicate one's political views or personality. "But what if surveillance systems can actually go under your skin as you are reading or watching it? Perhaps your TV is watching you and a biometric bracelet on your wrist is measuring your body temperature, your blood pressure, your heart rate. They can know not only what you are reading or watching but how it makes you feel."[11]

This is the world Dylan inhabits in our story. This is the *real-life* experiment running daily on our children. And by the way, the surveillance tech is only growing more sophisticated and better at what it does—by the day.

6

DREAMS BECOME NIGHTMARES

SHOW

What follows is a reimagining of actual historical events.

—

December 1, 1955. It had been a long day for forty-two-year-old Rosa Parks. A seamstress by trade, she had just completed her shift at the Montgomery Fair department store. Now she wanted to go home. Like other Blacks in Montgomery, Alabama, Rosa detested riding the municipal buses. They had a demeaning Negroes-in-back policy, which meant colored passengers had to sit in the rear, leaving the more desirable front seats to Whites.

Rosa tried to avoid those buses whenever possible. But on this cheerless winter day, Rosa's feet hurt so badly from standing for hours that she slipped into the middle row behind seats reserved for Whites. She didn't notice who was behind the wheel. If she had, she never would have gotten on the bus in the first place.

More than ten years prior, she'd had a nasty encounter with James Blake. Back in '43, Rosa had boarded a bus driven by him. As soon as she paid her fare, Blake had a command for her: "Don't just head to the Black section."

"What?" she asked.

"You better exit and then reenter through them back doors."

"Why?"

"That's the requirement for Black riders."

Humiliated, Rosa got off the bus to do as Blake asked. Then he drove off.

For the next twelve years, Rosa avoided the municipal buses. And if she hadn't been so sore and tired, she might have stayed off the Cleveland Avenue line today. Now seated, Rosa put her fingers to her throbbing temples. It was growing dark. Driving along, they passed a few Christmas lights outside people's homes. Their wan glow did little to penetrate the gloom. A cold gust of air escaped through the doors as more passengers boarded. Looking around, she could see the bus was nearly packed.

Her eyes fell on a White passenger at the entrance. A mistake. She quickly looked down, hoping nothing would come of it.

"You there!" he called to her. "You."

Rosa said nothing. She stared at the floor.

"Hey, girl. I'm talking to you."

A nearby White woman elbowed Rosa. "He wants you."

Rosa looked up to see the White passenger shouting. He pointed at her and three other Blacks seated just behind the White section. "Y'all better move it. You know the rules. You're in Whites' seats."

Nothing happened. It felt to Rosa like the other Black passengers were waiting for something. More cruelty. A reprieve?

"You hear him?" asked the White woman who had nudged her.

Rosa acted like she hadn't heard either of them. Then she saw the White passenger approach their driver. *Blake.*

Her heart sank. She wished she had never gotten on the bus today.

After putting the bus into park, Blake rose to his full height. "All right. All right." He pushed his way down the aisle, heading straight for Rosa and the three other Black riders. "Y'all know it's against the law for you to sit in the same row as a White on a city bus."

It was no longer cold on the Cleveland line. Or at least Rosa could no longer feel it. All the air had gone out of the room. She shot a quick glance at the three other Black passengers. None had moved to get up.

Their driver did not look happy about that one bit. "You'd better make it light on yourselves and let me have those seats," said Blake.

At last, the other Black riders surrendered their spots. Not Rosa.

"What are you doing?" Blake yelled in her face. "Get up. Now."

Rosa met his eye. "No, sir," she said quietly.

She could hear someone behind her gasp. Maybe the White woman.

"I could fine you."

She said nothing.

"I could get you arrested."

"My feet are tired," said Rosa softly. "I'm not going anywhere."

Rosa glanced up to see a bulging vein in Blake's forehead. It looked ready to pop. Teeth gritted, he started to say something and then turned around. Minutes later, the police arrived to take Rosa to jail.

That night Rosa got the call.

The recently appointed pastor of the Baptist church, someone named Dr. Martin Luther King Jr., had a plan. "You're one of the most respected people in our community," he told her. "Your character is impeccable; your dedication is deep-rooted. You need to be the face of this."

"You mean the boycott?"

For some time, she had heard rumors of what Dr. King was organizing: Black people using their pocketbooks to protest racist Jim Crow laws.

"How we do business is the answer," Dr. King continued. "And with whom. Nonviolent, this is the most potent technique for an oppressed people."

"What do you have in mind?"

"We'll start this week. No more bus riding. Tell everyone you know. Instead, form carpools to go to work or to do your errands and shopping. No more spending our money in any White establishments."

"Even friendly ones?"

"Even friendly ones. Money can be our platform. Our voice when they want us silent. Can you even imagine what'll happen to this city when courageous Black brothers and sisters stop purchasing their bus fares?"

Rosa pictured her neighbors and friends walking alongside the Cleveland line. All those Whites riding nearly empty buses. "It'll send a strong message."

"It'll bring Montgomery to its knees. Without shots fired. Without any physical harm," said Dr. King.

—

It started December 5. Fully 90 percent of Montgomery's Black population stayed off the buses. Rosa's neighbor Ethel offered to drive her to work that day. Her husband, Richard, drove them to Rosa's house in his tan Packard. Ethel hopped out of the passenger seat after they pulled into the driveway. "This is for you. You earned the best seat."

Rosa waved her off with a smile. "No. No. You sit there. I don't mind getting in back—when my friends ask."

"I insist," said Ethel. "Besides, sitting back here means I don't have to hear Richard grumble about the price of gas."

"Well, it *is* quite high." Richard checked behind to ensure the road was clear before backing up. "We were hoping you might contribute to the cause," he added with a whisper.

Ethel kicked the back of his seat. "You don't think I heard that? We can't make Rosa pay for gas."

"Really, I don't mind—"

Richard patted Rosa on the shoulder. "You can pay next week."

"Next week?" said Ethel. "How long are we supposed to do this for?"

Rosa remembered Dr. King's words. "We're to boycott as long as it takes to change hearts and minds."

Before they could take Rosa to work, their Packard required gas. Richard swung into Hart's Full Service, a nearby Black-owned station. An egg-shaped sign hanging off a thin, rusty pole read, "Official Imperial Esso Dealer." Rubber hoses coiled up neatly against metallic pumps on an island between the two car lanes. Sunshine reflected off clumps of snow packed against the body shop.

The sight paired with Rosa's bright mood. Things were looking up ever since the bus incident. She didn't care so much that the cops had stuck her with a ten-dollar fine. Times were changing, and Black people were organizing. No longer must they abide racist laws that made daily life so nasty in the South. Dr. King was right. Blacks had the real power. Now it was time to use it.

"What's that smile I see there?" Ethel met her eyes in the mirror.

"Nothing. Just glad to be alive today," said Rosa.

Across the street, she noticed a small crowd forming outside Allied

Union Bank, another Black-owned business. A half-dozen men in shirts and ties had lined up beside homemakers with strollers.

"Morning, Mr. Richard."

They turned to see Kent, the Black teen who worked for old man Hart. As usual, he wore striped overalls and a cap. With a little salute, he peeled off a rubber hose from the pump and began filling their tank.

"Nice to see you again," said Richard through the car window.

"So handsome," Ethel whispered to Rosa. "I've always liked Kent."

Rosa agreed with her assessment. "Polite too."

Kent wiped down their tires before starting on the windshield with a rag. As he did, Richard went for his wallet. Rosa saw it held a crisp five-dollar bill. "Sure I can't interest you in contributing to our gas fund?" he asked Rosa, a twinkle in his eye.

Ethel kicked his seat again. "You stop it right there."

"Okay. No need to get physical."

As soon as Kent finished pumping and returned the gas hose, he appeared at Richard's window. "That'll be $3.36, please."

"Sure thing, young man." Richard removed the fiver from his wallet. Before he could pass it to Kent, it vanished in midair.

"What in the world?"

Richard opened his door to see if the bill had fallen to the ground. There was no sign of it.

"You see that too?" Ethel called to Kent.

"I did, ma'am, and I don't know what to make of it."

"Like some magic trick. You trying to pull something on me?"

"No, sir. I promise."

Flummoxed, Richard rummaged in his seat and scanned the dashboard. He even checked the glove compartment for the missing fiver, though Ethel told him that made little sense. "I . . . I don't know what to say."

Kent didn't either. When a green Dodge pulled up, he took the chance to excuse himself. Richard turned to Ethel, the twinkle gone from his eye. "That was all the money in my wallet. What'll we do?"

Ethel got out her pocketbook. "I got seventy-five cents. It's something."

Rosa checked her purse. "I have seven dollars."

Ethel shook her head. "Honest to God, this isn't our sneaky way of making you pay. Right, Richard?"

Richard didn't respond. He was still looking through his wallet.

"I don't mind," Rosa reassured them. "Honestly."

Kent returned. He stood there waiting for Richard to say something. Rosa reached over him to hand Kent four one-dollar bills. Before she could, they also vanished. "What's going on?"

"Th-that can't be."

Rosa's hands trembled. It didn't make any sense. *How could money just disappear?*

"Did you just see that?"

All three in the Packard turned. On the other side of the island, a Black man had approached Kent to pay for filling up his Dodge. In his fist he held an empty wallet. "All my money," they heard him say. "Gone."

"I'll talk to Mr. Hart. He knows all you. You can come back later to pay," said Kent.

—

Minutes later they were back on the road driving through town. Richard couldn't stop shaking his head and muttering. "Just the darndest thing."

"How could it happen to that man too?" Ethel wanted to know. "And Rosa?"

Rosa wondered the same thing. It might be believable that they were all momentarily blinded from sun on snow. In that moment Richard might have dropped the bill, and they hadn't found it. But nothing could account for the money vanishing from her fingers *and* from the other man with the Dodge.

As soon as they passed Molly's, they knew something was wrong.

Through the café's window, they could see a sea of Black people going every which way in confusion. A couple were arguing with their waitress. Two men pounded their fists on their table. At the register, a crowd had gathered. Rosa couldn't hear what they were saying, but she had seen the same look on Richard's face today. Disbelief.

Richard slowed to a crawl. "Did the same thing happen here too?"

"Money disappearing for no reason," Ethel clucked her tongue. "It's like something out of Revelation."

Richard came to a full stop outside Allied Union Bank. By now the mass of people Rosa had first spotted at the gas station had swelled. Rosa had never seen anything like it. A long queue more than a hundred deep snaked past the parking lot and around an alley connected to a grocer. To the left and right all along Main Street, doors to Black-owned shops flung open. Black patrons poured into the streets.

That was when she heard the man with the megaphone speak. Bespectacled and middle-aged, he wore a vest over a white shirt with rolled-up sleeves.

He stood atop a ladder someone must have dragged before the bank doors. "I urge you to stay calm. We're doing everything we can to fix the situation."

Richard slumped over the steering wheel.

"You okay?" asked Ethel.

"That's what people say when they have no clue what to do."

"Where's our money?" a woman from the crowd shouted. Rosa could see two little kids beside her and the fear in the woman's eyes.

"He hasn't got it," a man answered her. "No one does. It's all gone."

The second he said it, the dam broke. The line at the bank surged, taking down the ladder along with the man on top of it. They stormed the doors, crashing through the glass. An elderly shopkeeper collapsed in the street. The mom with the kids covered her face and wept.

Rosa fell back in her seat. She had never felt so helpless in all her life.

TELL

In 2022, truckers changed the world with a mass protest. This is surprising, especially since pundits had assured us for years that artificial intelligence would render this occupation obsolete. Remember Andrew Yang's short-lived presidential candidacy?

A year before the pandemic, he campaigned on protecting truckers. By offering universal business income (UBI), he hoped to save them from job displacement due to AI advances. "All you need is self-driving cars to destabilize society," he predicted. "We're going to have a million truck drivers out of work who are 94 percent male, with an average level of education of high school or one year of college."[1]

Precedent supported Yang. A few years earlier, the meme "learn to code" went viral after journalists suggested truckers acquire new skills to compete in the Fourth Industrial Revolution. A 2017 article in the *Guardian* said truckers would soon vanish from our brave new economy. "For drivers like me, driverless trucks are the power loom and the sheepskin. There are about 3 million of us in the US alone (plus 600,000 in Britain), and we will soon be extraneous—roadkill, so to speak, except we won't be dead," wrote Finn Murphy, a trucker who had been driving since 1980.[2]

As it turned out, not only did trucker jobs *not* disappear, but also the humans performing these tasks remained central to daily life during the health crisis. Throughout the first two years of COVID, truckers stayed employed—and essential to the economy.

Media and politicians showered them with praise. Canada's Prime Minister Justin Trudeau tweeted the following on March 31, 2020: "While many of us are working from home, there are others who aren't able to do that—like the truck drivers who are working day and night to make sure our shelves are stocked. So when you can, please #ThankATrucker for everything they're doing and help them however you can."[3]

To the media and leaders like Trudeau, truckers were COVID heroes. Until they became COVID pariahs. What brought about the change? Political activism. Taking a page from Dr. Martin Luther King's playbook, they used collective action to bring Canada to its knees.

In the winter of 2022, Canadian long-haul truckers, also known as the "Freedom Convoy," protested governmental overreach concerning COVID-19. It's been estimated over fifty thousand trucks and more than half a million people turned out in freezing conditions to thwart Trudeau's health mandate. For weeks they gridlocked streets, honking horns, and hosting peaceful gatherings for other like-minded people. They refused to deliver food and other critical shipments, demanding that Trudeau relinquish his order requiring all Canadian truckers to be vaccinated or to quarantine on their return from the United States.

Trudeau did not take kindly to Canada's former heroes. Their actions angered him in much the same way boycotters in Montgomery must have upset Jim Crow despots. After trucker protests all but shut down the flow of goods in his nation, he invoked the so-called Emergencies Act. "You can't harass your fellow citizens who disagree with you," he said. "You can't hold a city hostage. You can't block a critical trade corridor and deprive people of their jobs."[4]

Then Trudeau went further. He financially deplatformed the rebel truckers. He made their money disappear. Invoking a War on Terror Law, titled the Emergency Economic Measures Order, his government required financial institutions (banks, credit unions, co-ops, and credit card companies) to cease "providing any financial or related services" to anyone connected to the Freedom Convoy.

Taking drastic measures not unlike those in our fictional story, Trudeau didn't just target peacefully protesting truck drivers. He went after "conspirators," concerned Canadian citizens who wished to express their solidarity with the movement, those who wished to contest governmental overreach.

Trudeau wasted no time disappearing their money too. He targeted the accounts of *anyone* connected to the protests. This affiliation could be as minor as a trucker's grandma submitting fifteen dollars to GiveSendGo in support. Because of her donation, this little old lady could expect the bank to freeze all her accounts; Visa would also cancel her credit card—effectively locking her out of society.

Much like China deplatforming its citizens for not falling into lockstep with carrot-and-stick digital incentives, Canada introduced a soft social credit system to the West. We should worry. Financial deplatforming is a terrifying threat not enough of us know about or care to fix. We do so at our peril.

The African American abolitionist Frederick Douglass knew this danger well. Like other enslaved children, he was taken from his mother when he was young. Owned by Captain Aaron Anthony, a wealthy landowner in Maryland, he managed to escape bondage. In a daring move, he slipped away in 1838 by posing as a sailor traveling from Baltimore to Wilmington, Delaware. From there he fled, ending up in New York. For the rest of his life, Douglass worked tirelessly to end slavery as a despicable abomination.

"Power concedes nothing without a demand," Douglass once said.

"It never did, and it never will."[5] He meant that tyrannical authorities, whether they were antebellum Southern states, police officers enforcing Jim Crow laws, or Canadian lawmakers imposing health mandates, will *never* give people their freedom just because we ask for it nicely. Instead, the people must demand their rights, fighting tooth and nail for each one. Sheryl Sandberg, Meta COO and author of *Lean In: Women, Work, and the Will to Lead*, said something similar concerning the struggle for female independence. "Social gains are never handed out. They must be seized."[6]

One way that disenfranchised individuals and groups go about advocating for themselves is via *civil disobedience* of the Rosa Parks variety. The Transcendentalist writer Henry David Thoreau coined this term in a famous essay. A couple decades before America's Civil War, the country declared war against Mexico in 1846. Like other critics of the conflict, he saw it as a cynical attempt to spread slavery deeper into the Southwest. (Thoreau had already ceased paying taxes years before to protest slavery, and the local tax collector had consistently looked the other way.)

Not this time.

That same year, the sheriff rounded up Thoreau and jailed him for his delinquency. While there, he wrote about the power of a person of conscience to act. "Let your life be a counter friction to stop the machine. What I have to do is to see, at any rate, that I do not lend myself to the wrong which I condemn."[7]

Catalyzed by Rosa Parks's bravery, Dr. King's civil rights movement, including his nonviolent tactics, largely came out of Thoreau's teachings. Back when he was still a college student in the 1940s, King read this same essay. It profoundly changed his life. As he wrote in his autobiography, "Here, in this courageous New Englander's refusal to pay his taxes and his choice of jail rather than support a war that would spread slavery's territory into Mexico, I made my first contact with the theory of nonviolent resistance. Fascinated by the idea of refusing to cooperate with an evil system, I was so deeply moved that I reread the work several times."[8]

Most of us grew up in a world vastly different from the nightmare Rosa Parks experienced in the Deep South. We weren't forced to give up our seats to someone else because of our skin color. We also didn't have to drink in separate water fountains or use segregated bathroom facilities. But the civil liberties we enjoy didn't come about because authorities *granted* them out of the goodness of their hearts. They were eked out through the actions of bold men and women willing to be beaten, imprisoned, even killed in the struggle.

These days, it's easy to forget a time existed not long ago when a Black man could be lynched for looking the wrong way at a White woman. Likewise, a young person of today lacking history may be inclined to believe that children of all races could always attend school together. But this reality only manifested because freedom fighters like Dr. King dreamed of a different, freer world.

On August 28, 1963, he delivered that vision at the steps of the Lincoln Memorial with these immortal words:

> I have a dream that one day even the state of Mississippi, a state sweltering with the heat of injustice, . . . will be transformed into an oasis of freedom and justice.
>
> I have a dream that my four little children will one day live in a nation where they will not be judged by the color of their skin but by the content of their character.[9]

Because we live in a nation of laws codified by our Constitution, Dr. King's beautiful dream became reality. But it wasn't a foregone conclusion. If the powers that be in the racist Deep South had had their way, they would have crushed Dr. King, Rosa Parks, and the rest of their movement. Driven by the same tyrannical impulses of Trudeau, they would have done all they could to destroy the freedom fighters' efforts to nonviolently advocate for themselves.

Of course, back then, racist authorities in the South didn't have access to centralized technologies, the type that can shut down someone's access to capital with a flick of a switch. But we must suspect that if they did, they would surely have used them. After all, "power concedes nothing without a demand," as Frederick Douglass said.

Accordingly, there's a reason we wrote this chapter in pure science fiction–style, imagining a past that never happened. We are all beneficiaries of history. Men and women of conscience fought to secure our rights. Blacks, not to mention every other marginalized group, could have lost their struggle for freedom, ushering in a nightmare scenario we can scarcely imagine.

Of course, freedom is not even a given once it's been wrested from the hands of tyrants. It must continually be fought for and sustained lest it be taken again. Decades after the civil rights movement, we are at an inflection point like no other in history. Over the years, tyrants have grown more polished and capable. They needn't sic dogs on protestors in the streets or spray them with water hoses to secure obedience.

No, they can be much subtler. As soon as the next would-be Rosa Parks dares to fight back, neo-tyrants can chop her down with one swift stroke: financial deplatforming.

The freedom convoy and its sympathizers aren't the only victims of this emerging tactic. It's being used against others who dare to push back. In the same year as the trucker protest, the mega payment platform PayPal cut off money to several left-wing media outlets, including *MintPress News*, *Consortium News*, and *Geopolitics and Empire* for questioning the mainstream drumbeat toward the war in Ukraine.

Each entity received a generic notice from PayPal stating that if they had any money in their account, they would be locked out of accessing it for 180 days. Afterward, PayPal would let them know how they could possibly access their funds—if they let them keep them at all. "We recently noticed an issue with your account," their letters read. "Because of this issue, your account has been permanently limited. We understand this may be frustrating and inconvenient, but you'll still be able to see your transaction history for a limited time."[10]

Notably, it's signed PayPal, not by any actual human.

The crime of these independent media organizations? Daring to stand up against the state's war propaganda. But PayPal's actions are also not without precedent. Julian Assange, another person who believes in collective action against powerful authorities, experienced similar financial deplatforming. In 2010, Visa, Mastercard, and PayPal blocked all donations to WikiLeaks.

Assange's crime necessitating the financial blockade?

Releasing ninety thousand files logging the true history of the war in Afghanistan, yet another disastrous military intervention the media supported in conjunction with the U.S. government, its military forces, and contractors. Assange's cache is considered one of the biggest breaches in military history. It included detailed reports on the coalition forces' attacks on civilians, questionable psychological tactics, as well as the many lies officials used to sell and prosecute the war.

These days, Julian Assange is far from powerful.

Like our fictional Rosa Parks, his ability to organize and resist tyranny has been utterly thwarted. Lacking money to continue his organization's efforts, much less mount an effective legal appeal for his supposed crimes, he languished in solitary confinement in London's Ecuadorian embassy for years. As of this writing, it remains to be seen if he will be extradited and tried under the Espionage Act.

There are those who don't think Assange should be released, let alone permitted to battle the forces of oppression. Likewise, there are those who don't side with the Freedom Convoy. For those who take this stance, let it be said that the particular issue at stake is not what's paramount. It's also not a Left or Right issue as it's been so often framed in the mainstream media. It's about liberty. And what matters most of all is that you comprehend how neo-tyrants are using centralized tech to crush the people, all of us penned up in our very own data plantation.

Still, you might say, "That's not my fight. Why should I care?"

It *is* your fight if you care to keep the freedoms you enjoy. For, as a wiser man once said, "Injustice anywhere is a threat to justice everywhere."[11]

PART II

SOLUTIONS

7

RUNNING DARK

SHOW

Wee-woo. Wee-woo.

Police sirens light up our car's console. Flashing red-and-blue lights splash across the leather interior, making it look like Christmas morning, although it's 4:00 p.m. in Rancho Santa Margarita. And July. At the same time Charles and I hear the shrieking din, giant monochromatic words pulse across the bottom third of our dashscreen: "Pull over. Police. Pull over. Police."

"Cavalry's a bit insistent," Charles says with a smirk. "Not likely to miss that."

"The dumb part is that they could *literally* pull us over," I tell my sixteen-year-old.

"Tractor beam–like. *Star Wars: Episode IV*. Too geeky?" he asks.

"Geeky? Yes. But spot-on."

Our Dodge is fully autonomous, though I'm driving it in manual. Connected to TheRoads' network, the cop easily could force us to the curb with the press of a button.

"Maybe he's just messing with your head. He could be mental himself. One out of twenty-two people are psychopaths. Did you know that?"

"I did know that."

But only because it's one of the many factoids Charles tells me daily. Gripping the steering wheel, I am struck by a dilemma. The go-along-to-get-along part of my brain admonishes me to edge us over to the shoulder beside the straw-colored chapparal and highway litter. The other part, the former class clown in me, urges me to floor it.

"Police. Pull over to the side." The voice blasts from our car speakers.

"Ho. They sound pissed, Dad. What'd you do?"

"Don't know. I wasn't even speeding."

"Did you fail to pass without properly alerting your fellow motorists?"

"Smart ass." A kid after my own heart.

"*Police. Pull over.*"

"All right. All right."

Signaling, my eyes land on our console camera. It shows two vehicles behind me in the outside lanes. Ignoring it, I peer over my shoulder to cut over.

"You can use the video stream, you know."

"You might. I'll trust my own eyes."

A little joke between us. Out of all the kids Charles's age, he'd be the last to rely on a driving camera. He's yet to be convinced life is a video game.

The second our tires crunch gravel off the 241, the cop wrests control of our vehicle. Working remotely, he steers us off the highway and toward the canyon hills. As soon as he kills our engine, all four of our windows roll down uniformly and the doors auto-lock, sealing us in. The glove compartment flips open, revealing its contents. Just my auto policy.

"Imagine if you had a gun in there," says Charles.

"Shut up."

Looking into my rearview mirror, I see the cop exit his vehicle and stomp toward us in knee-high boots. Across the dome of his helmet flash digital phrases like a billboard in Times Square: My name. My address. The date of my car registration.

The officer pauses before reaching my side. I can see he's checking something. "Body temperature scan tells me you're non-symptomatic. Even so, I'd prefer you to put on your mask."

Charles hands me my N95. I slip it on as Officer Williams continues. "No outstanding warrants. No tickets. Inoculations current. Sufficient carbon credits . . ."

With the window rolled down, I can hear the roar of cars whooshing by. It produces a warm breeze on my skin that isn't unpleasant. The sun beats down on the hot pavement, making it go all blurry at the vanishing point. A bead of sweat trickles down my forehead. I catch it before it hits the tip of my glasses.

"Your BAC is fine. So's your skin galvanic reading."

"You mean his tonic conductance is between ten and fifty, Officer?"

"I told you to shut up," I hiss at Charles.

Officer Williams flips up his helmet visor so we can see his blue eyes for the first time. They don't look amused. "What was that?"

I flash my son a look that says, *Now's not the time to be your usual cocky self.* Either he doesn't care or he doesn't see it. His grin goes all screwy like he's auditioning to be the next Joker.

"Why aren't you wearing a mask, son?"

Charles takes his time unrolling the one he keeps in his pocket for situations like this. He talks in his professor voice while putting it on. "As you know, Officer Williams, the sympathetic nervous system regulates the galvanic skin response, itself an indicator of emotional arousal. I assume your handy-dandy scan was just checking to see if my pa is all hopped up on goofballs." I shake my head in disbelief. "Which, I assure you, he's not."

"He's kidding, Officer. Not about me not being on drugs. That's true. I mean he's just being a smart-alecky teen. You remember what that was like?"

He says nothing. Just flips down his visor to cut off more discussion. For a good minute, he writes notes to himself on his tablet, presumably issuing me a ticket. I'm tempted to ask why, but I know better, so I just sweat in silence.

"Your email address still current?"

I tell him yes.

"That's where I just sent your citation."

"For what, Officer?" Charles asks.

"Your mask needs to be above your nose," he tells Charles. Then he redirects his attention to me. "As you should be aware by now, all California drivers must switch off manual mode by the July 20 mandate. It's unsafe to be on the road in a nonautonomous vehicle."

"Yes, of course. I was planning to."

"Anyway, it's only the 19th, Officer. We still have a day."

"Charles. *Quiet*."

Officer Williams flips up his visor. Squatting, hands on his knees, he resembles a quarterback barking huddle orders as he peers at my son. "My niece died in a car accident. She was only ten. An autonomous car would've saved her life. Now, is that funny to you?"

"Not at all, Officer. Neither of us think that's funny. Right, son?"

Charles says nothing. Neither does Officer Williams. It's a standoff. Finally, the officer rises to his feet, still glaring at us. "All California cars are required to be in fully autonomous mode as of July 20. Tomorrow, penalties begin."

His mask over his nose, Charles leans so far over he's practically in my lap. "So you didn't just write my dad a ticket?"

I pinch Charles. He pinches me right back.

"Oh, I wrote your dad a ticket. You can think of it as a pre-ticket. TheRoads have been alerted to your vehicle. Should your GPS coordinates display manual movement tomorrow, you can expect an auto-debit from your account."

"That's so convenient." I can see Charles's eyes twinkle with mischief behind his mask. *This kid. I swear.* "My dad won't have to even write a check."

"Watch it, young man."

"I have a question," Charles continues. "What if you're a California resident but you work in Arizona? Technically, you can still manually drive in other states. Can't you?"

Officer Williams leans in so close I can smell his cologne. At the corners of his mask, I detect a faint stubble growing. "Your name's Charles Stogel. Age sixteen. I noticed you have a driver's license. How'd you like it revoked?"

"He's sorry—"

Charles cuts me off. "*Revoked*? On what grounds? My galvanic readings don't portend drug use." I can tell by the way he talks that he's gritting his teeth.

Officer Williams looks equally pissed but restrains himself. Afraid to mop up the sweat pooling on my forehead, I let it drip down my chin.

"TheRoads can also track *motorists*," he says. "I'll be sure to flag you."

"Please, Officer. He didn't—"

Officer Williams holds up his hand for silence. He glares at Charles, heat radiating off him. "Heard of the no-fly list? They got that now too, for drivers."

He crunches gravel with his boots all the way back to his vehicle.

"Shouldn't have done that," I tell Charles.

He stares out the window as our car hums to life with the click of a few buttons from Officer Williams on his tablet. This time, I let the car's computer guide us home.

—

The thing you need to know about my dad is that he used to be a lot more rock 'n' roll and a lot less soft contemporary. If Pandora Streaming could assign personalities based on words and actions just like it recommends songs, it would label Pop something like *former hellion* or *milquetoast by design.*

Growing up, he wasn't all neutered and worried. Before Moms left, he was more chill about stuff. He laughed a lot. Took chances. Hell, back when we lived up in Marin, he enlisted me to blur out our license plate digits so we could fool the toll cameras into letting us pass free.

His dad had a serious pair, too. Crotchety old dude came up in Vietnam, so you know he didn't truck with big gov telling you what to do. Prostate cancer courtesy of Agent Orange'll do that to you. About the only thing Gramps liked to do near the end was guzzle Stags in the garage. He and Pop would twiddle on an ancient '78 Dodge Power Wagon for hours, Gramps' tongue unfurling in his wet mouth the more beers he killed.

Before long we'd be knee-deep into "good old days" territory. That's when Gramps would go on a memory lane tear. "Used to be you could stroll up to John Wayne Airport an hour before your flight and pay cash for your ticket. No Homeland Security–TSA biosecurity–Big Brother–corporate commie state telling you your business—"

"That's a mouthful, Dad."

"I'm serious. You could hang out at the gate and kiss your girl goodbye. Now you gotta be on the whole other side of the airport, lest Saddam Bin Laden blows you up with a dern shoe bomb . . ."

Now that I think about it, Pop might have lost his edge earlier than Moms ghosting us. Most likely it happened when Gramps died. Something flipped in him, and he just stopped "pushing back on the bull," as his old man would say.

I don't make it much easier on him, I know. But someone's gotta push back. Or else what? We all end up listening to Josh Groban in our khakis.

"You still mad?" I ask as our car corrals us through the SoCal suburbs on autopilot. We pass houses with fake palm trees and synthetic grass.

"You should be mad at yourself," says Pop. "You're screwed yourself."

The steering wheel retracted, our dashscreen shuttered, we sit facing each other.

"Poor Officer Williams," I snort. "A few decades earlier and he could've been born a jack-booted Nazi. Can't you picture him asking for your papers?"

"Ha-ha." He doesn't really laugh. "That gestapo just revoked your driving privileges."

Okay, he's right. It wasn't so clever to poke the bear, but it felt good.

"How long you think I'll be on their no-drive list or whatever?"

Pop shakes his head. "Don't ask me."

I peer out the window at the six lanes of traffic. Ninety percent of the vehicles don't even have windshields. They've converted theirs to vidscreens so the occupants can watch Netflix while cruising. Although I suspect some are watching porn. Can't be sure, though, since they're opaque as hell, like some anonymous corporate Irvine high-rise. Who even knows who's inside these cars? They could be empty. Or filled with zombies. They look like moving coffins.

"Pop," I start to say.

"Yeah?"

"Nothing."

—

As soon as we get home, I tell Charles to order dinner for himself. I'm done for the evening.

"What do you want? Pho?"

"Nothing for me. I'm not hungry."

He follows me into my home office. I curl up on the sofa, Whiskers in my lap, purring happily. Somewhere in the clouds of my brain a migraine is forming. Within an hour I'll feel the thunder and lightning.

"*Pop?*"

"Just leave me alone. Don't you have homework?"

"It's July."

"Then go play *Fortnite* or whatever." Rolling over, I peel off my socks and pants, preparing for the storm.

—

Staring at all those moving coffins on the ride home got me thinking. Instead of ordering up noodles, I head for the garage. Neither Pop nor I have spent much time here since Gramps passed. In the corner is the mini fridge that served as his bartender the last few years. He never kept food in there, unless you count black licorice strips in your food pyramid.

I kick open the door. To my surprise, a lone Stag remains. Looking up at a framed picture of young Gramps and his Saigon unit, I give the old salty dog a proper salute. Then I pop the top and take a long pull.

Belching, I throw out my feet, settling in the wobbly wicker chair. My legs shake in that frantic way that used to worry Moms so much. "Is that what they call restless leg syndrome?"

"No, Ma. Just nervous energy. From a genius." She dug that last part.

Dominating the room is a long black tarp. And under that tarp is a part of Pop he doesn't want to face. The Dodge '78 Power Wagon and all those long-gone days. Maybe Gramps had some vision for this hunk of junk. Maybe he was going to soup up the horsepower. Maybe he was going to prettify it to enter one of those muscle shows old men like to attend so much.

I really don't know. He never told us.

Killing my beer, I throw off the tarp on the driver's side. Our Dodge now has a fob that only requires you to say "on" before the engine hums to sentience. This ancient beast requires a key. Checking under the dirty rubber mat, I come up short. Nothing on top of the visor either, so I check the glove box.

Bingo. The key's attached to a rusty beer opener that's seen some action. Remembering movies like *Bullitt*, I insert it into the groove and twist. It revs to life with a satisfying roar. Something compels me to floor it. Jesus Christ. It's like some demented monster constrained in park.

"Charles?"

Oh no. Shirtless, Pop wobbles into the doorway, hand on his head. He looks like pain himself. "What're you doing out here?"

Seeing him alone reminds me of the moving coffins. It gives me an idea.

—

"This is a terrible idea," I tell Charles. "I can't believe you talked me into this. We have no plan."

"If it's so crazy, then why are you in the driver's seat?" he says with a smirk.

"Today is July 20. If they catch anyone on the road that's not in an autonomous vehicle, they'll be fined. Or worse," I tell him.

"Not if we make it to Arizona."

We're both in my garage. More specifically, we're both in my father's old Dodge *inside* my garage. Key in the ignition, car idling, we sit waiting. Everything we care about is packed in bags stuffed in our trunk.

"Okay, I'll drive," says Charles. "You get out."

I turn to my boy. Handsome, he exudes a presence. Just like his mom. And just like his mom, he's got an incorrigible streak miles long.

"You can't drive. You're being tracked now. And we don't even know if this car will run. I can't tell you the last time Gramps took it out."

"They're not tracking *me* necessarily. TheRoads is watching for autonomous vehicles to make sure they're switched off manual. But guess what? This car doesn't have any computer in it. It's running dark."

"Running dark . . ." I picture a vehicle coming down the road at night, no headlights on. "They could still track us on our phones."

Charles unbuckles. He gathers our devices and exits the vehicle. A second later, he's back empty-handed. "That settles that."

"Fine," I say. "Even if the police or whoever couldn't track our vehicle or our persons, where would we go? What would we even do?"

"I have no frickin' clue. Now get out."

"Huh?"

He opens my car door, unbuckling me. "Out. Shoo."

He takes the driver's seat, and I ride shotgun. Looking over his shoulder, he throws the car into reverse. Before we clear the driveway, something occurs to me. "Wait."

Six minutes later, after much rummaging and even more cursing, I return with the object I sought.

"What the hell's that?" Charles asks.

"A *Thomas Guide*."

"A what?"

"A map. Ever heard of it?"

Charles chuckles and puts us into gear. "Nope. But I like the new attitude."

"What's that mean?"

"It means it's about time you stop being so damn hangdog."

Then he guns it down the street. I won't lie; I slump in my chair. I'm scared the neighbors will report us for having a combustion engine.

"Holy cow!" says Charles.

Straightening up, I peek over the dash. At first, I can't tell what the big deal is. A familiar sight, it's just a bunch of cars in traffic.

"Don't you see?" asks Charles.

"See what?"

"The cars."

"Yes? I see them."

"They're not all . . . moving coffins."

I turn to Charles. "Moving coffins?"

Charles pulls alongside them. Still pointing, he draws my attention to their windshields. Then it hits me. All down the street, cars have their vidshields down. They're driving manually. Like us. Their cars are also stuffed with suitcases and bags.

A girl Charles's age is at the wheel in the car beside us. She turns to look at my son, and her face lights up.

"Headed for freedom too?" she asks.

"Maybe we're not so alone."

TELL

Whatever you think of the 1991 action flick *Point Break*, there's a seminal scene with bearing on this conversation. At one point the main baddie, a surfer named Bodhi (played by the late great Patrick Swayze) gives a pep talk to his fellow surfers/bank robbers about why they should keep pursuing their endless summer adventure: "This was never about money for us. It was about us against the system. That system that kills the human spirit. We stand for something. To those dead souls inching along the freeways in their metal coffins we show them that the human spirit is still alive."[1]

Metal coffins. Sounds like our story. But first, let it be known that by no means do we condone bank robberies. Or encourage FBI agents to pose as cool undercover surfers to take them down. We are, however, aligned with Bodhi's sentiment on the sustained assault on the human spirit. We worry about what will happen should those who kneel at the altar of safety soon dictate our lives.

Now to driving.

More than any other icon, the car represents the American way of life. There's a reason so many songs celebrate it: "Drive My Car" (the Beatles), "Picture Me Rollin'" (Tupac), "Get outta My Dreams, Get into My Car" (Billy Ocean), and "On the Road Again" (Willie Nelson), to name a few. Why do so many teens like Charles long to get their license the second they turn sixteen? It gives them a taste of freedom. For the first time, they can go anywhere they like; they can be masters of their own fate.

This is made possible because of the sense of control that driving affords us. Of course, automobiles aren't just tools to get us from point A to point B. They represent something *symbolic*. And that might be just the big reason so many authoritarians are eager to see us safely ensconced in our metal coffins. Driving represents freedom—freedom that's under fire.

The movie *Point Break* came out in 1991. Decades ago, it predicted humanity's coming *neuterization* (in its own cheesy yet appealing way). It wasn't alone in depicting a way of life that's fast disappearing. Blustery action flicks of the 1980s and 1990s, like *Tango and Cash*, *Lethal Weapon*, *Die Hard*, and *Big Trouble in Little China* also conveyed a *joie de vivre* that's being quashed by a growing furor to stamp out all forms of risk in our culture.

The philosophy behind it is called *safetyism*. According to the Association for Psychological Science, quoting the *New York Times*, "Safetyism, a term first used in the book *The Coddling of the American Mind*, by Greg Lukianoff and Jonathan Haidt, denotes a moral culture in which people are unwilling to make trade-offs demanded by other practical and moral concerns. Rather than seeing safety as one concern among many, it becomes a sacred value."[2]

Lukianoff and Haidt's book explains the concept by reflecting on another term that's exploded into popular usage: *antifragile*. The polymath Nassim Nicholas Taleb wrote about this in a business book by the same name published in 2012. According to Taleb, things in the world may be classified into three categories:

- *Fragile:* vulnerable to volatility, uncertainty, or disorder. An example is the expensive china cup perched on your ledge. You bump into it and it's forever ruined.

- *Resilient:* something that absorbs disorder and stays the same. An example is the Jell-O in your plastic cup. When a minor earthquake strikes, it makes the Jell-O shake, but it remains unharmed or damaged.

- *Antifragile:* that which gains from volatility, uncertainty, or disorder. For example, people are antifragile. Life's stressors, like lifting weights, can build our muscles, making us stronger.[3]

In *The Coddling of the American Mind*, the authors discuss the rise of peanut allergies to show the dangers of an overabundance of caution in our culture, the dangers of safetyism. According to Mathew Lesh, for *Quilette*:

> From the 1990s, parents were encouraged to not feed children peanuts, and childcare centres, kindergartens, and schools banned peanuts. This moratorium has backfired. The LEAP study (Learning Early About Peanut Allergy) found that not eating peanut-containing products during infancy *increases* allergies.... Our immune system grows stronger when exposed to a range of foods, bacteria, and even parasites.[4]

Now, might the push toward autonomous driving cars be a similar case of safetyism? An overabundance of caution leading to bad results? To answer this, consider the messaging we've received on the need for self-driving cars in recent years. The *Conversation* reported in 2018, "The statistics measuring how many crashes occur are hard to argue with: More than 90 percent of car crashes in the U.S. are thought to involve some form of driver error. Eliminating this error would, in two years, save as many people as the country lost in all of the Vietnam War."[5]

Sounds like Officer Williams's rationale, doesn't it? Similarly, the book *AI 2041: Ten Visions for Our Future* by Kai-Fu Lee and Chen Qiufan presents a fictional tale about a future in which self-driving cars have replaced 99 percent of the cars on the road. Like TheRoads in our story, all autonomous vehicles are jacked into a digital hive mind controlling their movements.

In one scene from the story, a character named Zeng Xinlan explains why this is necessary for the maintenance of the utopian risk-free society Lee and Qiufan envision:

The smart control system decides which available car to send and calculates the optimal path to take based on the passengers' location and walking speed, to maximize airport efficiency and reduce passengers' waiting time. The road we're on right now is specifically designed to accommodate autonomous vehicles. The smart sensors installed along the road communicate in real time with the control system on every car and the traffic management infrastructure in the cloud, to ensure safety and orderliness.[6]

To reiterate, for years pundits have urged us to adopt self-driving cars. Employing appeals to safetyism rhetoric, they have warned us of all the crashes that happen annually, all the lives that might be saved if we just halted our selfish ways. Except that cars don't merely provide us with excitement or novelty; they offer us freedom, the ability to go where we want—without someone else's approval. Without being tracked and monitored.

We needn't look any further than what happened in 2020 for evidence of what's in store for us should we succumb to the push to eliminate our autonomy. If you'll recall, at the beginning of the COVID-19 pandemic, freedom of movement came under fire—in the name of safety from the coronavirus.

As *BBC News* reported on March 27, 2020, several individuals in the United Kingdom's Derbyshire were stalked by surveillance drones for the crime of exercise. "A force that released drone footage of people walking in the Peak District has been accused of 'nanny policing.' . . . Officers said travelling to remote areas for exercise did not count as 'essential travel' as permitted under government lockdown rules."[7]

To be clear, state authorities, not unlike our Officer Williams, decided that the safety of the United Kingdom's citizens was jeopardized by the actions of several people "walking their dogs and taking photos" and chose to stalk them, screaming orders from the sky until the bad citizens returned to their homes.

This was not an isolated incident. *CPO Magazine* reported on a similar government overreach that occurred in the United States one month later, citing the same safetyism rationale. According to writer Alicia Hope, the drones came equipped with similar invasive technology that Officer Williams used to surveil Pop and Charles before ever reaching their vehicle. "Apart from enforcing the social distancing rules, the drone manufacturer said the surveillance drones could track people with fever, high temperatures, heart, and respiratory rates using specialized sensor and computer vision systems. The drones could also identify people coughing and sneezing in crowded public places. According to the manufacturer, the drones could detect these conditions at a distance of up to 190 feet."[8]

Technological advances of the Officer Williams's variety are already employed by authorities to use at will on the public. In China, police use so-called smart helmets to take the temperatures of pedestrians as they patrol streets. Likewise, a January 2022 Human Rights Watch report states, "Greece is planning a new police program to scan people's faces and fingerprints that is inconsistent with international human rights standards on privacy and likely to amplify ongoing discrimination. . . . Under the EU-funded program, the police would use hand-held devices to gather biometric information from people on a vast scale and cross check it against police, immigration, and private sector databases primarily for immigration purposes."[9]

According to this same report, the police will soon possess smart devices not unlike Officer Williams's tablet to "scan vehicle license plates, collect fingerprints, and scan faces. People's biometric data can be immediately compared with data already stored in 20 databases held by national and international authorities."[10]

Based on these chilling developments, it's not a far leap to imagine a day whereby a state like California mandates autonomous driving for all citizens. Why? For your safety, of course. Then just like TheRoads, the state would be free to use its hive network to surveil all citizens, cutting them off from their ability to travel should they step out of line.

Again, for your safety.

Should we surrender to the self-driving vehicles scheme, it will be more than just a symbolic defeat. Not only will any authority be able to literally stop us from going anywhere at any time; it will also weaken the human spirit, showing us that we really are no longer in control of our destiny.

But we do have a fighting chance. The most powerful force we have on our side is not technological at all. It's the *human will*, the impulse to resist tyranny. More powerful than any innovation, it's our strongest weapon in the battle against technological tyranny.

It's been said courage is contagious. Bravery on display is what Pop and Charles experienced at the end of our story. Conditioned to believe they had no hope but to surrender to the mandate requiring they give up their mobility, they learned a surprising truth. The people hold the power. Once enough of us say no, their system of control, the most ambitious and authoritarian the world has ever known, will crack.

Then, little by little, sunlight will pour in, showing us the way out of our digital bondage.

8

#INIQUITOUS

SHOW

Harley Lockhart grew up singing Fleetwood Mac in the shower. Also in the car. At school. And everywhere else.

Stevie Nicks, the band's charismatic lead singer, was her hero. Like her dad, Harley loved Nicks's haunting lyrics. Really, though, Harley just loved words. Other high schoolers spent lunch gushing about sports and rumors. She stalked the campus, running poems through her head. It helped take her mind off what happened last year.

T. S. Eliot: *I should have been a pair of ragged claws / Scuttling across the floors of silent seas.*

Rumi: *The wound is the place where the light enters you.*

Despite her recent aloofness, Harley wasn't unpopular. Not at all.

"You're lucky," her little sister, Joss, often told her. "All the guys like you."

Football players crushed on her hard. So did the smarties in debate. Girls fancied her too. Emmie, her scene partner in *Our Town*, kissed her once in rehearsal. "I've been wanting to do that for weeks," she'd said.

Harley's grades were good enough to earn her a Duke scholarship, but she turned it down at the last second to move west. Staying in Denver was too hard. Too many memories.

"You can't go to Cali," Joss told her. "I'll never see you."

"Once a big label signs me, I'll be rich. I'll pay for your flight. You can come see me anytime you want."

"What about Mom?"

"Her too."

Breaking into the music scene didn't go like Harley expected. She grew up hearing tales of sleazy managers who made stars put out to launch their careers. At least that was what her dad had warned her about back when he still played.

In her head, she pictured a short, middle-aged guy with a gold chain. A receding hairline. Ford didn't fit that profile. He looked more Ashton Kutcher than Danny DeVito. And was sweet as pie on her Insta. "Caught you singing 'Heaven.' Dope. Great lyrics."

That was the first song she wrote. The full title was "In Love with Heaven." It came from a dream she had about getting to see her dad one more time.

But Ford wasn't her only fan. She couldn't believe the reaction she got online. The simple video she took on her phone strumming a guitar in her Venice flat was *fire*: 10 million views the first week, 80 million by the second.

"Gave me chills," said one commentor.

"Magic," said another.

"When's the album drop?" asked someone else.

Harley wondered the same thing. Never one to doubt herself—this was the same girl who'd beaten out all the dudes for Battle of the Bands—she expected representation.

She just didn't think it would come in the form of Ford.

"Wanna meet in IRL?" went the DM he sent after she dropped two more songs on TikTok. "Coffee's on me."

They met at Literati in Brentwood the next Tuesday morning. Exiting her Uber outside the café, she walked smack into a surfer-looking young guy with a mohawk and shaved sides.

"Wanna buy my album?"

She looked down. At his feet, she saw stacks of homemade-looking CDs with the printed label of a stuffed tiger.

It depressed her. *I can't end up like that.*

"It's called Hobbes. Like *Calvin and Hobbes*," he said. "To Calvin, Hobbes is a real tiger. To everyone else, he's just a plush toy. Get it?"

Harley believed in karma, so she handed him a twenty and walked off as fast as she could.

Entering the lobby, she passed aspiring screenwriters banging away on laptops. Lying-in-wait actors brought Niçoise salads to their tables, continually checking their phones for callbacks.

Ford didn't exude their desperateness. Not in the slightest. His "boy next door" handsomeness sucked her in like a straw. His dark brown eyes twinkled as he stood to greet her.

"Got you a mocha." He handed her a paper cup.

"Sorry, I don't drink coffee. Shoulda told you—"

Not skipping a beat, Ford handed the drink to a ponytailed young woman at a nearby booth. "Want this? It's never been drunk."

"Um, sure," she said, admiring Ford long after he returned his attention to Harley.

"You didn't have to get me anything." Harley sat down beside him.

"It's nothing. And you . . . you're everything."

Some sleazy Colonel Parker–esque record manager could never pull off a line like that. Ford could. He really was gorgeous.

Careful, Harley.

"You're my kind of musician," he continued. "Singer-songwriter. Like Nina Simone. Joni Mitchell. Memphis Minnie."

"You know Memphis?" Harley's eyes widened.

"'Course I do."

"Prove it."

"Prove it?"

Ford sat back in his chair. He looked stumped.

"Thought so." Harley crossed her arms. "You don't have to try to impress—"

He sang "When the Levee Breaks" at the top of his lungs, eyes closed. All around people stared. One guy got his phone out to video the performance.

"Stop it. You're crazy." But Harley couldn't help laughing. She liked him.

"Zeppelin borrowed Memphis's song. Honestly, I like their version better."

"Me too," she confessed.

Ford leaned forward conspiratorially. "So. I'm not just a fanboy. I work for KMF."

Everyone knew KMF Rights Management. They were huge. "You do?"

"I'm kinda like their eyes and ears for new talent. I brought them Romeo Dyson last year."

"Shut up."

She loved Romeo's Memphis trap, the way he let instruments—808 basses, kick loops, tape keys, synths—do the heavy lifting in his raps.

"Found him on TikTok." He smiled. "Like you."

It took all her willpower to keep her face neutral. "And what might KMF do for me?"

"Everything. Everything that matters. Production. Manufacturing. Distribution. We've got massive reach with media. Spotify. Facebook. How'd you like to be on the cover of *Rolling Stone*?"

That had been her dad's dream. Before he gave up playing. Her pulse quickened, but she stayed calm, her voice even. "People still read that?"

"'Course they do. And I know just how to put you on their radar. How'd you like to headline with Romeo?"

"Romeo? But his style's totally different. Like Drake. And I'm more like—"

"Christine McVie?"

"I was gonna say Stevie Nicks."

"Same difference."

She wanted to argue this point, but he was on to the next.

"We'll smash your two sounds together," he said. "It'll be sick. Think: Amy Winehouse teaming up with Ghostface Killah on 'You Know I'm No Good.'"

She liked that song. She also liked where this was going. She looked around at all the other wannabes eager for their big break in this town.

Could this really be happening to me? Could this be my life?

"You're gonna be huge. I know it. We'll build your brand off Romeo's." Ford put his hand on hers. And kept it there.

—

Before June started, #Iniquitous blew up like a hand grenade. Influencers hyped the concert on socials as *the* musical event of the summer. Tickets sold out in hours. Concertgoers would soon descend on the Hollywood Bowl.

The one person who wasn't so thrilled? Harley.

Even if Ford didn't look like he had to pay for sex, it didn't mean his offer didn't come with strings. She learned this *after* the ink dried.

It began with minor affronts. Like the time he took her shopping on Rodeo and insisted on accompanying her into the dressing room.

"Not a big deal," he told her. "Just wanna make sure your skirt fits."

"Can't you do that *after* I come out?"

He backed down with his same (sexy) smile. "Sure, sure."

Then at the Chateau Marmont shoot, he was all hands. Hand on her thigh in the limo up Sunset Boulevard. Hand on her shoulder when she met the photographer. Hand on her breast when she changed clothes. *Hand on her ass when they hugged goodbye?*

She decided not to tell her mom. She'd only worry. And remind her that she turned down Duke for this. So she called her sister.

"Don't throw it all away," Joss advised. "Okay. Okay. He's kind of a creeper. But I saw his pic. He's *hot*. And he's opening doors for you."

Yeah, but at what cost?

"He didn't say you had to, like, *do* anything with him, did he?"

"No. No."

"And he did hook you up with Iniquitous, right?"

Iniquitous. Harley almost said something more but cut herself off. She didn't want to sound ungrateful. "Yeah . . ."

"Look. You know I got your back. If he ever, you know, tells you he expects more, I'll be there in a split second. I'll kick his butt myself. *Promise.* But if it's just like this little stuff and you're on your way to mega-mega stardom, I'm not sure you should rock the boat."

"He touched my ass."

"He *did?* That's not cool. You must say something next time."

Only the next time Ford and Harley met was in a chaste KMF boardroom where there was no chance he would #MeToo her. Instead, he spent the meeting agreeing with the suits that "In Love with Heaven"—along with all the other songs she wrote—didn't belong on her debut album.

"But that's what got me noticed in the first place. All those people on Insta liked what I wrote."

"Of course," said the one female exec in attendance. She actually wore a pantsuit. "We just feel that with the whole Iniquitous-Romeo concert on the horizon, we should tweak your sound. A bit."

"Tweak—like how?" Harley asked, turning to Ford to back her up. For once he kept his twinkly eyes lowered.

That was when they sprung the ghostwriter on her. Harley didn't know people like him existed. At least not in the music realm.

"Jerrund's gonna help you," said a different suit. "He's the best."

A painfully thin man with tattoo sleeves on both arms loped in. His lips were gaunt too, the top one almost nonexistent.

"Super creative guy," said Lady Pantsuit by way of intro.

Jerrund handed Harley a stack of music sheets with completed lyrics. "I worked with Taylor."

"She *loved* him," said Ford. "And he's got tons of ideas for you already."

Harley didn't return his smile. It felt like the walls were closing in on her.

"You can write the next album," Ford assured her. "After your *Rolling Stone* cover."

"But—"

Harley tried to push back. That is, until Lady Pantsuit showed her where in her contract it said KMF controlled all content decisions. For the next five years.

—

#Iniquitous lived up to its hellish name. It began with sinister-looking memes on Insta featuring a picture of "bat boy," straight out of a cover from *Enquirer*. Someone in PR had superimposed Romeo's face on his. Harley was there too, her face airbrushed, surrounded by what looked like demons.

"It doesn't mean anything," Ford told her. "It's provocative. Everyone does this stuff for clicks."

The stage show pushed the theme harder. The marketing team insisted on a Burning Man–sized effigy of an owl with haunting eyes. Scantily clad dancers gyrated beside it. They alternated between worshipping at its feet and shooting stage blood at the audience with Super Soakers. Behind them, a painted backdrop featured devils torturing naked people in novel ways. A postmodern Boschian nightmare.

Harley tried to ignore the macabre aesthetics. How they dovetailed with the duets she and Romeo were to sing that night that came straight from Jerrund's twisted brain. Laced with graphic depictions of violent sex, they made Harley sick wondering what her mom would think. Or her dad.

Days before the show, Harley broke down on the phone with Joss. "I just can't. This isn't me."

"It's gross," Joss agreed. "I can't believe Ford's making you do this."

Harley wanted to tell her it wasn't just Ford. It was all of KMF, the geniuses who had mapped out her whole music career. She couldn't picture Stevie Nicks being told what to sing about.

"Don't come," Harley flat-out told Joss.

"But it's your big show. Mom already bought my ticket."

"I'll pay her back the money. But please. Don't come."

It required three more calls—and three times as many texts—to get Joss to agree to stay away. "But Mom and I are still gonna livestream it. You can't stop us."

Harley threw herself into work so she wouldn't think about that. She memorized Jerrund's songs. She went to rehearsals. She learned her dance moves. She did the press junket. She tweeted what Ford told her to say. She wore the skintight leopard leather pants he insisted on. The snug halter top.

The night of the concert arrived.

As Harley went onstage, she took a deep breath. Thousands of people stared back at her in the vast amphitheater, their phones pointed up at her. Instead of thinking about them or Ford or Jerrund or Joss, she saw her dad in her mind's eye. How he smiled at her before leaving the house that night.

"Yo, we doing this?" Romeo whispered behind her.

What if I just sang my own song? Who would stop me?

But she knew the answer. KMF would crucify her. Beginning with legal. Ford already told her that she could expect a lawsuit of "biblical proportions" if she veered off script.

The synth beats kicked in. Then the drum machine. The crowd cheered. They were ready. And she was ready for them. She would not be a slave.

She opened her mouth to sing "In Love with Heaven."

Then changed her mind.

Everyone said the concert was a success. Ford most of all.

"You're a *star*." He handed her a champagne flute in the limo home afterward, his hand on her thigh.

One success begot more success. She graced *Rolling Stone*. Then *Vogue*. Then *Time*. "The New Face of Music," ran a headline. "The IT Girl," ran another.

—

Five years later.

The venue is far from the size of the Hollywood Bowl. In fact, the intimate nightclub can scarcely hold more attendees than Literati's lobby.

Harley speaks into the mic. "You're my real fanbase. And the only ones who can claim that you now own Harley Lockhart's first independent album."

Cheers from the crowd.

Harley presents an old-school record. Her eyes flick past a QR Code and text reading, "Get your exclusive NFT access now," available on her private site. Below is a picture of her dad teaching her the guitar when she was six. She can't remember which song. Probably something by Stevie Nicks.

For a second, she flashes back to that day at Literati when she saw the surfer dude with his album. The picture of Hobbes on the CD cover.

He had it right. Surfer dude may have never been on the cover of *Rolling Stone*, but he also never sold out. At least that's what her dad might have said.

She begins to strum the first guitar strings, and the crowd quiets down. They lean in closer to hear her play the first few chords of "In Love with Heaven."

"This is for you, Daddy," she whispers.

TELL

On November 21, 1955, a then twenty-year-old Elvis Presley signed an agreement with his manager, Colonel Tom Parker. According to PresLaw, a site dedicated to making "available information on the Elvis-related lawsuits in a single location," this contract was not unlike the fictional one Harley signed. "The terms are extremely favorable to Col. Parker and give him pretty much complete control over Elvis' career. The entire contract is definitely very much biased to the Colonel."[1]

Elvis was by no means the only performer to be pressured into signing an agreement affording their representative vast power. Music biopics like *What's Love Got to Do with It* depict the savage way Ike Turner, ex-husband to Tina, mistreated her in his supervisory role. After plucking her from an abusive home, he got her to change her name from Anna Mae Bullock and then launched her career via extreme micromanagement, even violence. At one point he beat her with a shoe stretcher and scalded her with coffee when she was pregnant.

Like Ike, other managers used their authority to control their performer clients. R&B artist Chris Brown publicly rebuked his former manager Tina Davis for trying to harm him. Reportedly, he fired her after being manipulated by her for years, beginning when he was still a minor. In 2014, he tweeted, "My old manager is leaking my NEW album music and refused to give me my back up hard drive to sabotage my album. That's F'd up G!"[2]

Controlling managers have also sought to exercise authority over their clients' livelihoods and creative decisions. In 2019, the *Guardian* reported the Killers' lawsuit against ex-manager Braden Merrick for "'multimillion-dollar damages in concerts and lost touring revenues, and via the bungling of merchandising and promotional opportunities.' They also accuse[ed] him of working for the band's label, Island Def Jam, as a consultant without their knowledge or consent."[3]

Such power asymmetry has been all but baked into the business of creativity, no matter the field. We can call this the Intermediatory Model, and it's persisted for centuries, a practice whereby artists have had to rely on managers, publishers, agents, labels, and the like to break through.

Leveraging inexperience or naiveté, business-minded individuals or companies exploit creatives, especially of the newbie variety. The phrase "read the fine print" speaks to this issue and how legal teams have long preyed on the less than savvy to produce contracts unfairly tilted in their favor.

This is what happened to the Sex Pistols. According to *Lateral Action*, they didn't earn much on their first album because of their manager Malcolm McLaren's appropriating money intended for them. "John [Lyndon, a.k.a. Johnny Rotten] bounced back with the excellent and innovative band Public Image Limited [PIL]. . . . However ten years down the line he found he still owed Virgin Records money and PIL were not allowed to put any more records out until he paid back what was owed."[4]

To this point, Eleven B Studios recently broke down the three major ways record labels "screw artists."[5] These include:

- Not allowing them to own music masters
- Requiring 360 deals
- Demanding recoupment on all costs

Once upon a time, a positive sum relationship model existed between music artists and management, but now this dynamic hardly exists, if at all. Gone are the days when the former could enjoy as much as 15 percent in royalties from a single or an album. It made sense back then for performers like Johnny Cash and Metallica to accept less than stellar terms to establish their careers.

We can think of this period as Music Centralization 1.0. It began to collapse around the time Napster decimated the music label model in the early 2000s. At one point, approximately sixty million web denizens were sharing pirated MP3 files. Suddenly, music was free—*okay*, stolen—hurting artists and labels alike.

This didn't last long.

The 2001 landmark case *A&M Records, Inc. v. Napster, Inc.* sided with the plaintiffs. According to History.com, "District Court Judge Marilyn Patel issued a preliminary injunction ordering Napster to remove, within 72 hours, any songs named by the plaintiffs in a list of their copyrighted material on the Napster network."[6] It was only a matter of time before Napster collapsed, leading to Music Centralization 2.0.

In the wake of legal action taken against illegal file sharing, emerging platforms like Apple Music saw their chance to capitalize on chaos. Sitting on mounds of cash it could use to seize market share, it began buying up music rights. Other well-heeled tech intermediaries like YouTube, Tidal, and Pandora followed suit, leading to today's uncontested juggernaut: Spotify.

It now leads the world in clicks, eyeballs, and listens.

Boasting more than 150 million premium subscribers—not to mention those who use the free service—Spotify's centralized power and reach is unprecedented. As *Rigorous Themes* reports, "Spotify is used by almost every top musical artist in the world. That means with the app, you can access every new release. Spotify has about 70 million songs in its catalog compared to the 30 million that Pandora features."[7]

This brings us full circle.

Even if Colonel Parker exploited Elvis, at least The King could call his manager on the phone to talk about the problem. Today's musicians have no such recourse. Veritable digital serfs toiling away for their faceless shareholder masters, they must grin and bear financial subjugation for their art.

Jacobin puts the incredible bilking in stark, quantifiable terms. "Every time an artist's song is streamed on the platform, they are paid, on average, about $0.004, or just under half a cent. If they want to see a literal single dollar, then the song needs about 250 plays. Which, naturally, is difficult to achieve without considerable promotion."[8]

But the likes of fictional KMF are not long for this (creative) world. At least not if DeCent, as in decentralization, has its way.

DeCent is coming for the music industry in the form of non-fungible tokens (NFTs). "NFTs are 'one-of-a-kind' assets in the digital world that can be bought and sold like any other piece of property, but which have no tangible form of their own," according to *BBC News*. "The digital tokens can be thought of as certificates of ownership for virtual or physical assets."[9]

In our story, Harley doesn't know about NFTs or how to use them until after she is exploited for five years by a fictional label and a handsy manager. Like many vulnerable artists keen on rising to the top, she has little leverage or say over her future, especially if she ever hopes to break into such a competitive field. In essence, gatekeepers like Ford and the army of suits he works for turn her ambition against her—making her play ball for her career.

But the resolution of our story is no make-believe happy ending. It suggests precisely where the music industry—and every other creative field—is going. Once upon a time, artists needed middlemen like publishers and labels to reach the public. This is no longer the case. Anyone can self-publish a book on sites like Lulu, Blurb, Scribd, and, of course, Amazon. Likewise, anyone can release their song or album via sites like TikTok or YouTube.

What's been missing was the technical infrastructure to directly sell artistic expression to audiences. We can think of NFTs as certificates of authenticity. They can never be copied, but they can be transferred, returning artists to the driver's seat. This is especially helpful for tomorrow's creatives like Harley. As *GearNews* explains, "The most common use of NFT for musicians would be exclusively released albums and singles. But it can take many other forms such as concert tickets, images, contracts, handwritten lyrics, custom sound samples, and more. Public distribution of these items helps to ensure transparency and keep things honest by preventing tampering and fraud, perpetuating the attributions of rights, and tracking transactions."[10]

Even better, individual proof of ownership, validated via an immutable blockchain, promises to transparently provide an accurate and discernible transactional record. This means no more skimming off the top by greedy managers or labels. It also portends no more middlemen.

As we saw, Harley suffered from an imbalance of power. Gatekeepers, enjoying centralized control, pressured her to adhere to creative decisions she abhorred. They held all the leverage. At least they thought they did.

In truth, they did not. You see, the KMFs of the world lack something: the creative spark. Yes, they can be wonderful managers or representatives, liaisons negotiating on their clients' behalf. They can even nurture and develop talent. But they aren't the talent.

And the future doesn't belong to intermediators. It belongs to the Harleys.

9

WHAC-A-MOLE

SHOW

"This is gonna sound so fan-girly, but I don't care. I've crushed on you for *years*. Like seriously, for years. Ever since Occupy."

Demi Cadano smiles back in her professional, guarded way. A TV host herself, she's learned to not put much stock into what others tell her. Especially when she's being filmed—like right now. Camera ready, Demi sits on a soundstage across from Cherise Templeton, cohost of NBC's *FOMO*, America's favorite daytime talk show. A necessary evil.

The other cohost, Betts Ponds, sits beside her, sharing in Demi's interview. "Oh, please," she razzes Cherise. "What were you? Six back then?"

Laughter from the studio audience. They eat up banter between the dueling hosts. It makes for good television. It makes Demi nauseous.

"You can be a precocious six-year-old. Drew Barrymore? *Hello?*"

says Cherise. She's the blond one with the model looks. Betts wears the glasses that make her appear the intellectual. Demi wonders if her lenses are real.

Either way, the crowd cheers Cherise on. They like the salvo. *Will Betts volley back?* She does. Leaning in close to Demi as though Cherise can't hear her, she stage-whispers, "Self-confessed millennial here. I was there with you."

A screen on the dais flashes to a candid shot of a younger Demi in a gray fedora at Occupy. She's surrounded by a crowd of other twenty-somethings in Zuccotti Park. Many sport homemade signs reading, "We are the 99 percent."

"You totally pioneered activist journalism. How's that feel?" asks Betts.

Demi hates questions like this. She hates shows like this. "Well, I wasn't alone. There was Tim Pool—"

Cherise cuts her off. "Super modest. *Love it.* You see now why I crush on her so hard?"

Betts beams, recrossing her legs beneath her pencil skirt. Demi knows the network must have told her and Cherise to dress like that. Ratings.

"Okay. So what was all that like?" the latter asks. "Dish about Occupy."

Memories rush back to Demi. All those angry young people like her. Shafted after the 2008 bailout saved AIG but left them twisting in the wind.

"It was after 9/11," Demi begins, a story she's told often. "For years, all my generation heard about was terrorism. And war. War in Iraq. War in Afghanistan. War in Libya. No one was talking about the war on us."

"I like that." Betts turns in her chair to face the audience. "She's good."

Demi waits for the applause to die down. "Did you know the federal government changed it so that college students can't discharge their debts in bankruptcy? It happened in '76 when Congress amended the Higher Education Act. That means that a white-collar junk bonds broker can get his credit card charges dismissed in court if he runs them up—yet not the eighteen-year-old who had to go into debt for college just to get a job. Occupy Wall Street was our revolt against a system that turns us into modern indentured servants."

"You're totally right." Cherise points to Demi in the video image behind them. "Totally right. But I wanna talk about that fedora you're wearing—"

"Reminds me of Indiana Jones," says Betts.

"It does. You're right!"

"Now, was that a conscious choice to channel Harrison Ford?"

The cohosts lean forward, their elbows on their knees, doing their best impressions of intrigued journalists.

Demi counts to five before answering. "I just grabbed something on my way out the door that morning. My boyfriend had it hanging on his rack, and it was cold, so I took it."

It pains her to remember Ed, the computer programmer. The antithesis of Indy Jones. Her life that might have been, if only he had shared her same passion to save the world. She stuffs down the memory and steels her gaze.

"Sure." Betts pulls her back to reality. "You didn't know it would become, like, your brand?" Betts points to the fedora Demi wears now. "Come on."

Demi despises the catcalls on that zinger. She's grasping her chair handles so tightly her knuckles go white. *Don't you want to know where I went to journalism school, you insipid twats? Don't you want to hear that I was one of those broke students up to my eyeballs in debt?*

Except she doesn't say that. It would make the two bimbos' heads explode. Better to play the long game. Remember why she came here today.

"I don't know about all that." Demi touches her hat. "I just try to be me."

"Well, it's working. Like a charm," says Cherise. "You just made the jump from YouTube celebrity to NBC anchor. How many times has *that* happened?"

"Never. Unless you count Megyn Kelly. Oh, wait. She did that in reverse."

"Snap!" says Cherise to knowing audience laughter.

"Seriously, though," Betts goes on. "Why do you think your little YouTube show gets so many eyeballs?" *'Cause "journalists" like you and Cherise are a disgrace. Because you and all the other overpaid lackeys like you* are *nothing more than spineless shills, regurgitating government talking points.*

Except she doesn't say that either. It would thwart her plans. Instead, she crosses her jean-clad legs with the mildest of facial expressions. "I can't say. It's impossible to know what'll connect with the public—"

"It *is?*" Betts cuts in. "Tell that to marketing. Am I right?"

Calmly, Demi continues, "However, I do think there's a hunger for long-form conversations on pressing topics. Take the success of Joe Rogan—"

Cherise holds her nose. "Old horse dewormer himself."

Buoying audience laughter.

Demi ignores it. "Or any other podcaster. Sam Harris, for instance. They're having substantial discussions on complex issues you just can't conduct in a sound-bite culture of gotcha journalism."

Neither Cherise nor Betts can think of anything to say to that. Betts finally breaks the awkward silence. "Okay . . . so, like, what's something you covered long-form style on your YouTube show?"

Channeling her inner Edward Murrow, Demi ignores the smug way Betts baits her. She pauses for another five seconds and then answers. "Sure. Take quantitative easing—"

"God bless you," says Cherise to vapid laughter.

"Um, it's pronounced *gesundheit*," Betts mock-corrects her.

Demi presses on. "Most people aren't familiar with this economic term."

"Oh, I am," says Betts. She pauses dramatically. "I think it refers to an old, old wooden ship."

"*Anchorman!*" Cherise high-fives her.

Demi waits for the audience to calm down. "Quantitative easing is what the government employed during the Great Recession. Essentially, it printed money out of thin air to prevent too-big-to-fail banks from insolvency. Never mind the fact real people were hurting. Losing their homes, losing everything."

"Sad." Cherise shakes her head.

"Quantitative easing is also what brought on hyperinflation in 2022."

"So this is Biden's fault?" Betts asks. "But I thought you were a liberal . . ."

"It happened under *both* recent administrations. Left and Right. From February 2020 to March 2021, total circulating cash, mutual funds, and banking deposit money supply shot up from $15,473 to $19,896 trillion."

"Cha-ching."

"Right. But injecting that much money into the economy had real-world consequences. *Bad* consequences. The more money we printed, the less it was worth. It devalued the dollar, screwing over middle America even worse."

The audience doesn't know how to react to this.

"Miss Doom and Gloom over here. Am I right?" says Cherise, provoking nervous titters from the crowd.

"Oh, I love it," says Betts. "Demi's one smart cookie. We need more strong women like Demi. Am *I* right?" Good cop to Cherise's bad, she starts clapping. The audience joins in. "That brings us to today and your new show: *The World with Demi Cadano*. Tonight's your big premiere. Nervous, sister?"

—

Demi needn't have been nervous. Her new prime-time show clinched all the key demographics: men, women, young, old, Right, Left. The accolades poured in as tens of millions of viewers tuned in.

"Demi speaks truth to power. No lies," they said.

"Hard-hitting."

"She asks the questions no one else will."

"She says the things no one else will."

"She's not partisan. She holds both parties' feet to the fire."

"Demi can't be bought. She's the only trusted name in news."

So many good reviews eased her misgivings about going corporate. For years, she had railed against the Keith Olbermanns and the Sean Hannitys on her YouTube channel. "Fake journalists—they'll say anything to keep being invited to Martha's Vineyard and the White House Correspondents Dinner."

It bothered her to be playing the corporate game. But she had bills to pay. Not to mention, her plan: Wake up the masses—on the left *and* right.

She did it. Night after night, her show managed the impossible. It told the truth. *The World with Demi Cadano* exposed the real uniparty apparatus behind the false Right-Left mirage.

"Follow the money" was what her reporter heroes Woodward and Bernstein said when breaking Watergate. She took their advice. Using confidential sources in high places, she showed people how affluent interests pursued their self-serving agenda while distracting the public into political party tribalism. "Republican. Democrat. It's no different than Coke or Pepsi. They're just labels serving the same masters."

Demi's show was so refreshingly honest that it drew in apathetic TikTok-ers by the bushel. Even the jaded sub-Reddit crowd caught it. Nightly, she tied together all the faceless, soulless entities that had long collaborated and commiserated, holding the nation ransom, looting the treasury, bankrupting the middle class, eviscerating the environment. They cheered her on as she exposed Big War, Big Tech, Big Pharma, Big Finance, Big Health, Big Psychology, Big Prison, Big Food, Big Retail, and most of all, Big Government.

One night she got so heated about all the lies and mendacity that she went off script and started paraphrasing the late comic George Carlin: "The politicians are there to make you think you have freedom of choice. You don't. You have owners. They own the corporations. They've bought and paid for the congress, the state houses, the city halls. They've got the judges in their back pockets, and they own the big media companies, so they control almost all the information you hear. It's a big club, and *you ain't in it*."[1]

Amazingly, that was not what killed Demi's career. September 11 did.

On September 11, years after the first attack on the Twin Towers, a different form of terrorism brought first the nation, and then the world, to its knees.

It began as a denial-of-service assault on financial institutions. Users logging in to pay their mortgages received an alert that their bank's site was down. Same for credit cards. ATMs stopped functioning as they were knocked offline. POS machines in stores no longer worked.

The damage spread from there. Utility companies halted service. People's homes and businesses were without electricity. Gas shut off.

Water stopped flowing. Hospitals lost power and had to resort to gen-
erators. Las Vegas went black. So did Manhattan, Los Angeles, and
Chicago. Before the day was out, even streetlights stopped working,
leaving neighborhoods dark.

The next morning, a fraction of power was restored. The internet
still ran, but sporadically and inefficiently. Anyone who could get their
TV to work received the same emergency broadcast with these unfor-
gettable words: "We are under attack. This is not a drill. Repeat: this is
not a drill."

Months later when the dust finally settled, the world order had
shifted. "Total 911" was what the event that ended the old financial
system came to be called. Terrorists had hacked the accounts of bank
deposit holders, wiping out the savings of millions in seconds.

In response, the UN, along with the G7 countries, issued a global
Central Bank Digital Currency (CBDC). "We can no longer trust that
individual nations can secure their own money supply. The looming
dangers of insurrectionists bent on undermining our way of life has
forced us into collective action. All money, now in the form of CBDCs,
shall be regulated by a centralized and global authority."

Demi returned to the air. Shaken by Total 911 and the harrowing
weeks without power in upstate New York, she was relieved to be back
in the studio. At least it offered a semblance of normalcy. Shivering
nightly beneath blankets, eating cans of cold tomato soup, and worry-
ing someone might break into her house had nearly driven her insane.

She lost ten pounds, and her hair had thinned. When airports were
finally operating again, she took a flight to Baltimore to bury her father.
"He wasn't made for a world like this," her seventy-nine-year-old mom
told her. Somehow, her mother had survived, living in the same house
as her dead husband through the cold, hungry nights until help came.

Despite all that horror, Demi felt it was her duty to resume broadcasting. The first night back on *The World with Demi Cadano*, she

looked pale and too thin, but so did most of her audience. "We've all been through a shock," she began. As she read from her teleprompter, her throat tightened. An image of her mom in her pajamas cradling her dad popped in her head. "I'm sorry..."

The engineer on the other side of the camera shot her a look, wondering if they should scrap what she just recorded and start over.

She pressed on instead. "No one can say the last few decades have been *orderly*," she began. "First, there was 9/11, then the Middle East wars, torture revelations, high school shootings, police brutality, the 2008 collapse, White-on-Black police brutality, the 2016 contested election, George Floyd protests, COVID-19, January 6, and so on. Chaos has been the state of the world all my adult life. Perhaps yours too. We've known nothing else. And yet I am worried. More worried than I ever was through all that. Most of all, I fear what'll happen now that the United States has signed the Global Governance Treaty subordinating our national sovereignty."

NBC fired her the next day. They issued a statement explaining her dismissal. Three sentences stood out. "In this unprecedented era of uncertainty and danger, we cannot risk misinformation and disinformation. The stakes are too high. We wish Ms. Cadano the best in her career..."

Undeterred, Demi returned to her "little" YouTube channel, known as *The Demi Show*. Appearing with no makeup, she went back to wearing her fedora. Lacking camera operators, she recorded the whole thing on her phone.

Topic one? NBC's dismissal. "I would like to begin by saying what just happened to me isn't special. It happened to Phil Donahue. MSNBC fired him for not going along with the second Iraq War. RT pushed out Abby Martin for criticizing Russia's takeover of Crimea. They'll tell you I'm the next Alex Jones. The next Steven Crowder, the next Tucker Carlson. It doesn't matter. Yesterday they were removing leftists; then it was rightists. Now it's anyone who doesn't go along with the program. Anyone who's spreading misinfo and disinfo is a threat to their power."

YouTube didn't bother with a warning. They just yanked Demi's account. *Poof*—her video library gone. All seven years of her work memory-holed.

She jumped to Rumble next. "Hello, friends. You're tuned in to *The Demi Show*. I'd like to begin with a question you may have asked yourself in recent weeks. 'What can I do if I am told my digidollar isn't accepted as payment?' This is no idle query. One of my listeners wrote to tell me that because of her county's lockdown laws, it's illegal for her to buy things in a different city. Her money doesn't work. Not at the grocery store to buy food for her kids. Not at the gas station to purchase gas to get home. First of all, my heart goes out to her. This is just the kind of problem we take on here at *The Demi Show*."

Before the week was out, Rumble received so much pressure that it, too, booted her off. She moved on to BrandNewTube, another video-sharing platform.

"Hello, friends, you're tuning in to *The Demi Show*. Today, I want to talk to you about the new Global Pandemic Treaty. Did you know all participating nations must require their citizens show proof of vaccination?"

BrandNewTube canceled her show. So did the next dozen video-sharing platforms. Word was out that Demi was content poison, a propaganda insurrectionist. No channel would host her after AIbots used facial recognition to seek out her online presence like a digital heat-seeking missile.

At least the owners of these platforms were apologetic. "We're sorry. We love your show. We appreciate what you're doing. We just can't let the government cut off our digidollars."

"Don't you see?" she would say. "That's how they want to control you. The only way we can mount a defense is by telling people what's going on."

"We're with you in spirit," they'd always say. "But our hands are tied."

—

One night Demi finds herself back in Zuccotti Park. It's all but deserted. Passing a couple in masks keeping their distance, she can't help recalling how crowded it was in those heady 2011 days. Over there was once a drum circle where kids in dreadlocks and men in suits jammed together. On the far side, she can still picture the makeshift stage they set up. She recalls grabbing the bullhorn to recite her poem: "Risen."

An ode to Christ, it was about how the evilest forces on earth can never defeat the one true God. "And they won't beat us now," went the last line. Shivering, alone in the park, now with autumn's leaves swirling around her, she wonders why she ever wrote that. She's not even Christian.

Like most people, Demi saw her bank account shrink after Total 911. It never really came back. Still, she has enough CBDCs to buy a beer by herself in a sad sports bar at happy hour.

Falling back into a booth, she aimlessly eats stale nuts from a little plate. She glances up at the TV. There's one in each corner of the darkened room. Each is set to a different game. The one she's watching shows a basketball match—the Lakers versus the Knicks. It looks normal enough.

Unless you peer too hard at the fans.

"They're all deep fakes. Precaution against super-spreaders."

Startled, Demi looks up. It's her boyfriend from the Occupy days. "*Ed?*"

"You're not an easy person to find."

"You were looking for me?"

He points to her hat. "You took my fedora."

"You lent it to me, remember?"

"Not for that long."

"What do you want, Ed?"

"The same thing I wanted then. I just didn't know how bad things would get."

Demi takes her hat off and shakes out her hair. She feels old. "That's nice. It's over."

Ed lifts his chin, indicating the TV. "I used to like watching your show. Too bad they canceled it."

"'They' canceled *all* my shows."

"They've got you on the run, huh?"

"So you heard?"

Ed takes a dozen nuts from her plate and spreads them across the table.

"Hey, I was eating those."

"You ever play the game Whac-A-Mole?"

"What?"

"This is a crude demonstration, but it'll work. There are twelve nuts here. Try to get them all off the table."

As soon as she pulls a few away, he adds more from her plate. She's never fast enough to get them all off before he adds more.

"Amusing game, Ed. I'm gonna head out."

"Wait. What if I told you there's a way for your show to return online? And stay online?"

Her eyes narrow. "How?"

"Same concept. Whac-A-Mole. Distributed on a crypto-enabled blockchain, we can move faster than the AIbots. Every time they take you down, we'll just move your show to a new platform. A new domain."

"It's got to be more technical than that."

"It is, but would you really care if I told you how the back end works?"

"Not really."

"All that matters is you stay one step ahead of the Whac-A-Mole. Even better, no one can take down your video library. There'll be an immutable decentralized record."

Still the professional, Demi hides her growing excitement. "Money?"

"Blockchain supports that too. Every subscriber can pay us in micropayments."

"Micropayments?"

"Think of them like tiny subscription fees. Only they don't run off CBDCs. We don't transact at all in *their* economy. We use a decentralized exchange."

Demi leans back in her chair. She puts her hat back on and slides it down her face. "What are you trying to do, Ed? Save the world?"

He eats all twelve nuts off the table. "I'm sorry I didn't come to the park that day. I should have."

Sighing, she gets up to go. Before exiting, she turns around with a grin. "Hey, Ed. As soon as we get this show going, I'd like to change the name."

He grins back. "No more *The Demi Show*?"

"Nah. Let's call it *Disinfo and Misinfo with Demi Cadano*."

"I like the sound of that."

TELL

In the spring of 2022, the Department of Homeland Security announced plans to assemble a "Disinformation Governance Board." DHS Secretary Alejandro Mayorkas told CNN it would function as follows: "What it will do is gather together best practices in addressing the threat of disinformation from foreign state adversaries, from the cartels, and disseminate those best practices to the operators that have been executing in addressing this threat for years."[2]

The so-called Disinformation Governance Board is by no means the only attempt to shut down free speech in the name of protecting the public from what the government deems as lies. In 2018, the bill H.R. 3359 amended the 2002 Homeland Security Act to redesignate the DHS's National Protection and Programs Directorate as the Cybersecurity and Infrastructure Security Agency (CISA). According to Congress.gov, "Its responsibilities shall include: leading cybersecurity and critical infrastructure security programs, operations, and associated policy; and carrying out DHS's responsibilities concerning chemical facility antiterrorism standards."[3] Under Chris Krebs, the first head of the CISA, the organization's mission was to combat what it dubbed "misinformation and disinformation," often spread via social media and online communications.

Already efforts are underway abroad to similarly combat the spread of "misleading" online content by authorities. The European Commission, the executive branch of the European Union (EU), has stated its commitment to stamping out mendacious propaganda to protect its nations' "values and democratic systems." According to its site, it defines the problem this way:

> Disinformation is false or misleading content that is spread with an intention to deceive or secure economic or political gain, and which may cause public harm. Misinformation is false or misleading content shared without harmful intent though the effects can be still harmful.[4]

Like its American counterpart, the European Commission employs high-minded rhetoric to underscore its commitment to protecting constituents from consuming information that could sway their opinions and thought processes. "The spread of both disinformation and misinformation can have a range of consequences, such as threatening our democracies, polarizing debates, and putting the health, security and environment of EU citizens at risk."[5]

Laudable goals, no doubt.

But we must ask the question: Is it the government's role to police information from adults capable of making up their own minds? Republican Senator Rand Paul posed this query to Mayorkas during a Senate hearing in May 2022 following DHS's announcement of the governance board. Mayorkas countered by saying it wouldn't be his organization's job to police disinformation at scale, only "when there is a connectivity between disinformation and threats to security of the homeland."[6]

Never mind that the term *homeland*, which rose to prominence after the 9/11 attacks, smacks of Fascist Nazi Germany and all its horrors. Are we expected to believe that the government should act as our informational gatekeeper? The same government that assured us Iraq possessed weapons of destruction, thus necessitating a tragic, preemptive war? The same government that was exposed by the Pentagon Papers for having lied to the republic about the necessity of the Vietnam War—then lied insistently for years to keep the conflict going?

Senator Paul spoke for many of us when he told Mayorkas:

> Do you know who the greatest propagator of disinformation in the history of the world is? The U.S. government. ... I don't want governing guardrails. I want you to have nothing to do with speech. ... You think the American people are so stupid, they need *you* to tell them what the truth is?[7]

Fortunately, outrage against the proposed Disinformation Governance Board was so vehement that DHS had to scrap its plans weeks after its public announcement. Tellingly, none other than the *Washington Post* served as an apologist for the demise of the would-be Ministry of Truth.

Self-described journalist Taylor Lorenz wrote the column lamenting its demise, along with the resignation of Nina Jankowicz, its director, who was forced to step down because of immense public backlash.[8] (Among other things, Jankowicz engaged in her own misinfo/disinfo activities—for instance, denouncing the Hunter Biden laptop story in the *New York Post* as Russian propaganda, which later proved to be false.)

What's so interesting about Lorenz's elegy in the *Post* is not just the fact that she has historically taken aim at fellow journalists—for instance, at one point, doxing the creator of *Libs of Tik Tok*—but her rationale for the governance board's expiry:

> The board itself and DHS received criticism for both its somewhat ominous name and scant details of specific mission . . . but Jankowicz was on the receiving end of the harshest attacks, with her role mischaracterized as she became a primary target on the right-wing Internet. She has been subject to an unrelenting barrage of harassment and abuse while unchecked misrepresentations of her work continue to go viral.[9]

This pertains to our above story. According to Lorenz, right-wingers *alone* brought down Jankowicz and her Ministry of Truth. But the ACLU, a left-wing advocacy group, came out against it too. So did many left-leaning journalists, including Glenn Greenwald, Jimmy Dore, and Max Blumenthal of the Gray Zone.

Demi, our fictional broadcaster, worked hard to show the public that the Left and Right share much more in common than the media would have us believe. If, as George Carlin once said, "It's a big club, and you ain't in it,"[10] then the moneyed powerbrokers behind it can't all be left or right wing. They represent the interests of a *uniparty*, a contingent of well-placed individuals unbound by the false Left-Right dichotomy we are force-fed.

The fictional media bigwig Arthur Jensen (played by Ned Beatty) said as much in the satirical 1976 film *Network*, itself an indictment of the media: "You get up on your little twenty-one-inch screen and howl about America and democracy. There is no America. There is no democracy. There is only IBM, and ITT, and AT&T, and DuPont, Dow, Union Carbide, and Exxon. Those *are* the nations of the world today."[11]

Regardless of whether you agree with Jenson's cynicism, the outcome of the governance board's collapse is only—as of this writing—*temporary*. Mayorkas's DHS has only put it on "pause." We can expect that it will return, next time presumably with a more polished director unsusceptible to the same PR vulnerabilities as Jankowicz.

This is why we need decentralized tech alternatives to access information outside the state-sanctioned system. Thankfully, free speech–focused video-sharing platforms already employ peer-to-peer streaming tech to bypass censorship constraints imposed by the likes of YouTube and Facebook. Here are just a few alternatives from a growing list:

- *BitChute:* Under the direction of Ray Vahey, the company CEO who expresses commitment to First Amendment principles, this company decentralizes video distribution to resist Big Tech censorship. What's more, creators of the Demi variety can monetize BitChute videos using cryptocurrency in the form of CoinPayments.

- *GabTV:* Ad-free, this video-sharing hub is supported via member donations, not advertising. So far, it's pushed back on Germany's Network Enforcement Act and its efforts to fine the service for disseminating so-called fake news.

    "At Gab, we believe that the future of online publishing is decentralized and open. We believe that users of social networks should be able to control their social media experience on their own terms, rather than the terms set down by Big Tech," explains the company on its site.[12]

- *BitTube:* This video service is built on the Interplanetary File System (IPFS), a "peer-to-peer hypermedia protocol designed to preserve and grow humanity's knowledge by making the web upgradeable, resilient, and more open."[13] In practice, this means that the platform serves as a free speech conduit, in part by supporting magnet URIs. These permit resources to be shared without the need for a continuously available host, thereby circumventing central authority.

Of course, it should go without saying that *none* of these platforms is a silver bullet. Any could be co-opted or taken down at some point. What matters more is that we support and encourage a plurality of decentralized media services to combat the stranglehold of authoritarian control. Options breed options, the antithesis of the Disinformation Governance Board's attempt to gatekeep informational flow.

What's more, we must invest in the same kind of decentralized payment technology that Ed advocates for Demi to fund her alt video-sharing network. So far in this book, we have shown that the big payment players like Visa and PayPal have financially deplatformed news sites such as Wikileaks. As corporate consolidation increases and innovations advance, we can only expect more financial crackdowns against those who speak truth to power.

There's one more reason DeCent shows promise for the future of journalism: commerce facilitation outside any centralized currency exchange. In our tale, Demi gets set up to receive micropayments from loyal audiences to avoid the same fate as Assange and other targeted media outlets. This is just one mechanism for decentralized commerce, brought to us by the blockchain. We look forward to more that provide distributed peer-to-peer exchanges.

Even so, we advocate for greater diversity when it comes to even decentralized payment modalities. Again, options breed options.

Returning to the *Washington Post*'s one-sided reporting on the

165

failure of the ill-fated Disinformation Governance Board, we would be remiss if we did not observe how far free and open journalism has fallen. "Democracy dies in darkness" is the slogan of the newspaper Bob Woodward and Carl Bernstein once used to cover government lies in the form of Watergate.[14] It's since been bought by Jeff Bezos,[15] Amazon's CEO and one of the most powerful people on earth (listed as the fifth most powerful person by *Forbes*).[16] Is it any wonder the *Washington Post* now laments the latest state-run efforts to constrain informational flow and expression?

There's another quote contesting darkness we wish to share. More apt for the current age, it sums up our view on the coming struggle for the dissemination of truth in these challenging times. As the poet Dylan Thomas once said, "Do not go gentle into that good night, . . . / Rage, rage against the dying of the light."[17]

10

YOU WILL OWN NOTHING
AND BE HAPPY

SHOW

Cheng Ni began questioning things when they fined him for defying the energy lockdown. Strike that—they didn't *fine* him. The World Gov debited the digidollars from his digital wallet. But it was all the same to him.

What you should know about Cheng is that he isn't the type of guy to make a big stink. At least that's what his mom always said. "He's my sensitive boy. The artist."

Cheng parlayed that sensitive side of his into a modest artistic career. Rather than go into medicine like his mother wanted or become a lawyer like his father insisted, Cheng opened his own photography studio in Everett, Montana.

"And not just because of his photographic memory," Ju would say. That's Cheng's beloved wife.

They met in Everett, where they went to college together. Ju liked sweet but shy Cheng from the start, but she really came to adore the man Cheng *became*. He took care of her and did well for himself. His studio was nestled beside the nearby campus, and he benefitted from a lucrative university contract making him the vendor of choice for the school's many sports games and graduations. Plus, Everett happened to be a sleepy little town composed of many other young families. It seemed like each one always had some new birth to celebrate, some happy milestone requiring beautiful photos.

Like everyone else, Total 911, the global financial terrorist attack, took Cheng by surprise. Thirty-five years old at the time, he had lived through 9/11, the 2008 crash, and COVID-19, so he wasn't wholly unprepared for sudden crises.

But this was bigger, more impactful. To Cheng, time existed as pre–Total 911 and post–Total 911. First, he lost all his savings, plus all the money in his business checking account. So did pretty much everyone he knew.

Luckily, the world government was prepared. At least, that's how Cheng saw it. Within months, it announced a multinational treaty binding all nations to a common currency, digidollars, issued and controlled through the international body.

Cheng was grateful for that. All the money he had in his accounts swiftly returned, enabling him to conduct his business as usual with only minor hiccups. After that, if Cheng was being honest with himself, he didn't look too deeply into the political side of the attack.

Frankly, it didn't interest him much to understand who had done it or why. It could have been Al Qaeda or ISIS, even some of those domestic terrorist cells his brother Dheng often warned him about.

Cheng would humor Dheng when he went on his rant and then promptly forget the conversation. He had more important things on his mind; caring for a five-year-old and an eleven-month-old baby sucked up all his available bandwidth. Since Cheng's studio connected to his home, he also ran point on caretaking.

Ju, for her part, worked long hours as a traveling nurse, hopping from hospital to hospital as needed within the tri-county system. Her open-ended schedule allowed her to pick up more hours but was hell on stability. Always on call, she never knew which facility would need her from one day to the next.

Cheng, on the other hand, relied on Google Calendar and convenient scheduling apps to manage his busy day down to fifteen-minute segments. Between appointments, he checked in on five-year-old Esme's progress on ABCFriend, the handy remote learning interface issued from the school district. It connected to her smartlink, learning about *her* as she, in turn, learned to spell and read.

"That way, it's the perfect teacher," the school told him and Ju when their daughter first got her implant. "Personalized to every student, it grows *with* them as they pass from grade to grade."

Baby Kaia was too young for her own implant, of course, but she loved to look at the bright and colorful tablet screen, learning alongside her big sis. *World's most effective babysitter*, Cheng thought. *And free to boot.*

Free was an interesting concept to Cheng these days.

After the world economy crashed so spectacularly, he expected real economic pain: exploding gas prices, stratospheric food costs, and the like. That didn't materialize. Instead, he received unexpected—but not unwanted—notices from creditors informing him that . . . he no longer owed them any money?

Like free manna from heaven, these statements came, absolving his family from debts. The $41,000 Ju still owed on her med school loans? Forgiven. The $12,000 Mastercard bill containing the 100W

LED Monolight kit with stands and softboxes? Gone. His mortgage balance? Wiped out.

Even better, Cheng could now depend on monthly Universal Basic Income (UBI) checks for one thousand digidollars. That wasn't enough to cover all of life's expenses, not with two young kids to feed, but it didn't hurt either.

In many ways, life hummed along smoothly for Cheng and Ju that first year or so after Total 911. That is, until the Everett City Council passed Green Friday. "As your elected leaders," the bill went, "we are tasked with the responsibility of confronting our existential climate crisis. In consideration of our children, as well as future generations, it would be an abdication of our duty *not* to act in the face of crisis. Therefore, we are passing into law Resolution 2.15 ordering all citizens and businesses to lock down every Friday. It is our hope that the cessation of consumption will dramatically reduce Everett's carbon footprint. Let Everett be a model for other cities similarly concerned about eco-sustainability."

What that meant in practical terms?

As an essential worker, only Ju was allowed to leave the house on Fridays, and then only to go to her hospital job. The one time she stopped off for a Beyond Meat quesadilla at McDonald's, the DMV License Scan read her plate and debited her account for the infraction. (Essential workers were required to set appointments at essential businesses like McDonald's before visiting. No drop-ins allowed.)

Back to Cheng. Green Fridays meant losing one full week's worth of customers. That wasn't so bad. With the lion's share of his bills sayonara'ed, he didn't fret about lost revenue.

That is, until Green Fridays affected him in a different, more personal way. Three months into the new policy, Cheng woke up one summer day determined to enjoy the beautiful weather. "C'mon, Esme. C'mon, Kaia. Let's take a walk."

"Do I get to pick flowers?" asked Esme as she stepped into her sandals.

"Of course," said Cheng, dressing Kaia in shorts and a T-shirt. "We can pick roses from our yard—"

"And make Mommy a necklace?"

"Sure, if you want."

"I wanna make Mommy a rosie necklace. It'll be pretty."

Once the kids were dressed, Cheng placed Kaia in her stroller with her sippy cup and Rufus, her stuffed elephant.

"I steer," said Esme, taking over pushing duties as they exited their house into the June sun. It wasn't yet 9:00 a.m., and already Cheng could feel the warmth. Breezeless, it hovered in the air like a snuggly blanket. A Montana native through and through, Cheng knew that warmth would soon grow oppressive, trapping you beneath its covers with no chance for escape.

Good thing we're doing something about climate change, he thought. In just a few hours, Everett would become a fireball—and stay that way long after the sun set.

Looking back on that day, Cheng would be hard-pressed to say much of interest. It blended into life's dreamy background noise, neither entirely memorable nor forgettable. If asked, he might have mentioned strolling through the empty park or pushing Esme and Kaia on the swings before returning to their godsend of an air conditioner.

The only thing that stood out was picking roses.

And that was only because of what he received in his inbox minutes later: "It's come to our attention that you have harmed the environment," read the city notice. "As you know, we live in a complex ecosphere encompassing at-risk flora and fauna. Disturbances to the natural order can have deleterious consequences."

Cheng thought the whole thing must be some joke.

Until he saw a bird's-eye drone shot of himself and the girls picking roses from the hedges outside his home minutes earlier. At the bottom of the email was the Everett city seal. Just above that was written notice he would be charged one hundred digidollars for his infraction.

—

Cheng's heart raced so fast he thought it would burst out of his chest. He hated public speaking. As far back as elementary school, he had bad memories of the fear he felt approaching the blackboard. It didn't matter that he always knew the answer; he feared the twenty to thirty pairs of eyes glued on him. Irrational as it was, it made him feel like he was being swallowed up.

That was why it was way out of character for Cheng Ni to be standing before the six-member city council, not to mention surrounded by dozens more citizens who also came for their sixty seconds before the civic body. Somewhere in the back of the room sat Ju with their two girls, supporting him.

"Esteemed members of the Everett City Council," Cheng began, his voice cracking, "I come before you because of this notice I received." Cheng held up a printout of the email containing his fine for the rose incident. "Normally, I'm not a person to contest something like this. A husband and father of two, I've lived in our wonderful community all my adult life. I love it with all my heart. The last thing I want to do is make trouble."

Cheng had to stop. His mouth had gone bone dry.

Reaching down, he picked up and sipped the bottled water Ju had been so thoughtful to insist he bring with him. For a second, he caught the eyes of the board. No, they weren't swallowing him whole.

Instead, they seemed impassive. Bored. Cheng had the odd sensation he could pass into another dimension before their eyes, and they would merely go to the next citizen and their allotted sixty seconds for public comment.

"Um," Cheng resumed, "it's not that I'm against protecting the environment; it's just that I'm confused as to why I am not allowed to cut my own roses."

Buzz.

The timer beside him reached the sixty-second mark. Cheng felt relieved that this was over. He had said his piece. Now he could sit down and forget it all.

"Mr. Ni," said a city council member. "Can I see that email?"

Caught off guard, Cheng quickly handed it to the woman with a placard reading, "Deb Gomez." She was gray-haired, and her wrinkled mouth gave her a permanent scowl.

"I *thought* there was some mistake when you held this up." Mrs. Gomez leaned toward her male colleague beside her, pointing at the page.

"Hmm," said the man with the placard reading, "Craig Dellison." "Admins must have missed this one."

Cheng turned to look at Ju in the back row. She gave him a thumbs-up.

"Mr. Ni," Councilwoman Gomez continued, "as to your fine concerning the destruction of natural resources, you may file a formal complaint online. Processing times range from sixty to ninety days. Within that time frame, you can expect a written response concerning your contention. What I am more interested in is the time stamp on your printout. It appears you were outdoors on a Green Friday when the drone took this photo."

"Yes," said Cheng. "I was outside with my girls."

"Charming," said Councilwoman Gomez. "Except according to Resolution 2.15, all nonessential community members are not to leave their home on Fridays unless their activities are essential. Are you an essential worker?"

"No, but I wasn't at the store or anything—"

City Councilman Dellison cut him off. "Resolution 2.15 states that nonessential citizens cannot be outdoors at *any time* on Green Fridays unless an emergency warrants their egress. Was there an emergency at that time?"

"No, Esme and Kaia wanted to make a rose necklace for their mom."

"In that case, I move to submit that Mr. Cheng receive another fine," said Councilwoman Gomez to the others beside her, "this one for violating lockdown orders." She turned her eyes on him. "You may expect an additional debit from your account. Next public comment, please."

—

In the following weeks, Ju saw a change in Cheng. Furious at how he was treated—"in front of my family!"—he threw himself into his new project.

He was determined to know how it was possible for an American citizen to be treated this way.

His online searches took him to an article from several years back celebrating Everett's contract with GTS Services, a private defense company supplying video surveillance to local governments. This was the very same firm whose drone had captured him and his girls cutting roses that day.

Yet Cheng couldn't remember ever seeing a drone flying over his home or anywhere else on his street or in his town. *How did it capture me?* he wondered.

He found his answer a day later in an interview with GTS's CEO,

Mark Davies. Buried ten columns into a fawning Q&A in some trade journal was this startling line: "Our drones hover in low orbit, not unlike the satellites enabling global telecommunications. This benefits our customers from a nuisance perspective. I can tell you that no one wants to hear the grating noise of a drone's propellers over their back-yard, including me."

Cheng froze when he read that. It never occurred to him that drones could be spying on him 24/7 without his knowledge. *Could they be surveilling Ju and the girls all the time too? How much footage do they have on us?*

The next day happened to be a Green Friday. With Esme on her learning app and Kaia dozing, Cheng had time to answer his questions. Somewhere in the vast pages of Everett's labyrinthine website, he found language describing his rights (or lack thereof) as a citizen. According to everett.gov/FAQ202, Cheng's activities—and those of his family living—were construed as "data points" for "civic usage and optimization."

In plain English, anything he—or his family—chose to say or do in public were the intangible property of Everett. "Such information may be utilized for the safe and orderly functioning of our community and the collective good."

—

The following week, Cheng returned to the city council for another crack at public comments. Again, Ju and the girls sat in back cheering him on. Except this time, Cheng didn't feel shyness or fear. Indignation replaced them.

"I stand before the city as a concerned citizen," Cheng began. "Before this summer I couldn't tell you the names of any council members. I didn't even know this building was where city meetings took place. Now I can tell you the exact laws that say the people around here aren't people. We're *data points*." The more Cheng talked, the louder and madder he became. He turned fully around to face his fellow citizens. "Today, they're pulling money from our accounts for daring to step outside on Fridays. What'll they do next with our data? Punish us for *thinking* the wrong things?"

Buzz.

"Your time's over," said Councilwoman Gomez.

But Cheng paid her no mind. He hadn't prepared what he would say before coming here. He was so mad that he let loose. But a chilling notion just occurred to him. *Could the city monitor his thoughts as data? Or his family's?*

Alarmed, he whipped around to look at Kaia with a sinking realization. In an instant, he realized what he and Ju had done.

—

"As your family pediatrician, I don't recommend this procedure," Dr. Knox told Cheng and Ju. They were alone in his office. They had asked Dheng and his wife to watch their girls for this consult.

"Why not?" asked Ju, her arms folded across her chest, mama-bear style.

Dr. Knox pointed to an imaging scan of Kaia's brain. "Well, it's been a year since her implant. Since then, your daughter's been connected to the network, enabling her to better learn, just like her classmates, through her smartlink."

Cheng shivered, picturing an invisible drone in the sky watching Kaia, vacuuming up her thoughts to reward or punish her. "So, what would happen if we were to remove the implant?"

"Again, I don't recommend that—"

"We heard you already, Doctor," said Ju. "My husband's question was, 'What would happen if we did?'"

"Medical professionals have differing views on this. Some dismiss negative outcomes outright. Others believe them to be negligible. On the other hand, there are those who worry that without the digital interface, your daughter's academic progress could be stunted."

"Forget about her grades," said Cheng. "Will it harm her physically to remove it? Will it hurt her in any way?"

"No, I don't see why it would—"

"Then we want it removed," Ju ordered him before he finished his sentence.

Just then, Cheng received an alert on his phone.

It was another notice from the city: "We at Everett have a zero-harassment policy toward city officials. Due to your disorderly conduct at the recent council meeting, we will be auto-debiting your account by $500. We hope this penalty will discourage future displays of hostility toward elected officials."

—

The coming months tested Cheng and his family. Without warning, all of Ju's hospital engagements dried up. No explanation was given; she just stopped receiving appointments. Though Kaia wasn't physically harmed in any way by the removal of her smartlink, her schooling suffered. It wasn't due to any poor academic performance; rather, she received warnings from the district informing her that her nonparticipation was harming her grade point average.

"Never mind that the girl's in preschool," Ju said to Cheng.

"What are they saying the problem is?" he asked.

"They're complaining they can't access her data."

"You mean they can't read her mind?"

"Exactly."

But Cheng's finances took the biggest hit of all on the day he announced his candidacy. "I am running for city council for the same reason I come back weekly for public comments," he said in a video he posted on TikTok. "I'm no lawyer, but I went to school where I learned about something called the Constitution. It protects our property." At this, he recited the Fourth Amendment, which he still knew from heart: "The right of the people to be secure in their persons, houses, papers, and effects, against unreasonable searches and seizures, shall not be violated . . ."

He paused and then stared right into the camera. "I believe that our *data* is our property. Our intangible property. No city government, not even Everett, can seize or search our property. Especially one acting so unreasonably."

Cheng's business account suffered next. He got a notice from Global Bank—in partnership with the World Gov—that his funds were being frozen for an internal audit.

He didn't take this lying down. "They did this to me on purpose for no other reason than that I am stepping up. That I'm running for office, that I'm pushing back," he told his growing number of TikTok followers.

Things only worsened from there.

Cheng received notice that his many bills, including his mortgage and Ju's student loans, were suddenly being reactivated. "For violation of the UBI Covenant," he was told in an email. "Insurrectionist activities automatically nullify your access to debt dismissal."

That wouldn't be so bad except that Cheng's "insurrectionist activities" also disqualified him from receiving his one thousand digidollars stipend. Lacking Ju's income and with his debts mounting, Cheng worried how they could keep their home. If things didn't turn around, they would have to default on their mortgage. They would be out on the streets.

Cheng stopped sleeping. He stopped eating. He grew desperate.

One night Ju heard him sighing in bed and turned to him. "What is it, baby?"

"What have I done to us?"

His girls slept in the next room. Cheng could hear Kaia's gentle breathing via their baby monitor. More than anything he wanted to go in there, lie down with her, pull the warm blanket over them both, and make it all go away.

Ju hugged him. "You did what you had to do. For us."

Cheng said nothing for so long Ju wondered if he had fallen asleep. At last, he sat up in bed. Grabbing his phone from the nightstand, he turned it to video record, live broadcasting himself to his TikTok followers. "Fellow citizens of Everett, I want to pledge to you tonight that I'm *not* going away. No matter how much they try to intimidate my family or me, I will not give up. Not ever. Now I want to say something to my fellow Americans—all of you. More eloquent than me, the following words sum up my feelings."

Wiping away his tears, Cheng began in a choked voice that grew stronger with each word: "We hold these truths to be self-evident, that all men are created equal, that they are endowed, by their Creator with certain unalienable Rights, that among these are Life, Liberty, and the pursuit of Happiness. That to secure these rights, Governments are instituted among Men, deriving their just powers from the consent of the governed . . ."[1]

That night Cheng gained a hundred thousand followers. The next day he doubled that. By the end of the week, he was a million strong and counting.

TELL

On January 10, 2016, professor and founder/executive chairman of the World Economic Forum Klaus Schwab sat down with journalist Darius Rochebin in an interview for the Swiss Channel RTS about Schwab's predictions for the future. Below is part of their exchange:

> DR: Today, at the end of this, we are talking about chips that can be implanted. When will that be?

> KS: Certainly in the next ten years. And at first, we will implant them in our clothes. And then we could imagine that we will implant them in our brains, or in our skin. And in the end, maybe, there will be a direct communication between our brain and the digital world. What we see is a kind of fusion of the physical, digital, and biological world.[2]

What on earth could be the pretext of chipping people? How and why would anyone agree to such a thing? To answer this, let's return to the famous dictum of President Barack Obama's one-time chief of staff Rahm Emanuel: "You never want a serious crisis to go to waste."[3]

First, the crisis.

Throughout the previous chapters, a pattern of recent history emerges. In stark relief, we may discern that the most monumental events of the last twenty-five years share a common antecedent: chaos. The failed war on terror sprung from the deadly 9/11 attacks. The 2008 financial crisis occurred after the housing market crashed under the weight of foreclosures. And the devastating number of sicknesses, deaths, and lockdowns arose from our misguided response to the COVID-19 pandemic.

Now, the part about seizing opportunities.

Catastrophic, each of the above events produced tremendous fear, resulting in worse countermeasures. September 11 brought us the Patriot Act and the present digital surveillance apparatus. The Great

Recession led to quantitative easing as an economic tactic, paving the way for hyperinflation, the devaluing dollar, and recession. And COVID-19 established a pretext for vaccine passports and an emerging bio-security state.

COVID-19 also ushered in something worse: centralized techno-tyranny in the form of "the Great Reset." In 2020, three months after the United States locked down, Schwab published a book by the same name. He urged the acceptance of *stakeholder capitalism* after the coronavirus pandemic exposed "inconsistencies, inadequacies and contradictions of multiple systems—from health and financial to energy and education."[4]

In Schwab's own words, this crisis is ripe for opportunity. But for whom? "One of the great lessons of the past five centuries in Europe and America is this: acute crises contribute to boosting the power of the state. It's always been the case and there is no reason why it should be different with the COVID-19 pandemic."[5]

As in the past, the social rationale and political justification underlying such power grabs are based on the narrative of "countries at war" (only this time against an invisible enemy).

Schwab's solution to the crisis? The Great Reset. Here are its three stated goals:

1. Governments should improve coordination (for example, in tax, regulatory, and fiscal policy), upgrade trade arrangements, and create the conditions for a "stakeholder economy."
2. Investments should advance shared goals, such as equality and sustainability.
3. Innovations of the Fourth Industrial Revolution should be harnessed to support the public good, especially by addressing health and social challenges.[6]

All this seems innocuous—except when you look more deeply into the World Economic Forum's other messaging throughout the years. Not long ago, the WEF put out a video campaign with an image of a smiling young man and these words: "You will own nothing and be happy."[7]

Most anyone who sees this video for the first time would be confused. How could it possibly come to pass that (1) no one would own property anymore and (2) they would be happy about it? The very notion flies in the face of everything Americans have come to expect about their way of life.

And yet what the WEF is proposing could well come to pass. COVID-19's arrival has not only shown the precariousness of our global supply chain; it has also shown the world that all we have come to expect about daily existence could change in an instant. For instance, should we somehow travel back to 2019, the average person would be astounded to learn that within the year most local restaurants would be shuttered, businesses closed, and people confined to their homes.

Likewise, should they flash forward three years, they would be floored to know that China would lock down the entire city of Shanghai and their pets would be murdered out of "safety precautions." Then, when the starving, screaming citizens begged to be let out of their skyscraper cells, a flying drone would appear in the sky to warn them off, saying, "Please comply w[ith] covid restrictions. Control your soul's desire for freedom. Do not open the window or sing."[8]

None of this would seem possible not so long ago. And yet all of it happened. Now, as we come to the close of our book, we want you to expand your mind as to what is possible. Not what you would like to happen, but what could happen if we do not wake up like Cheng and Ju. If we don't advocate for ourselves.

Like many of us, Cheng lived a comfortable life before Total 911. The crisis disrupted his way of life but didn't destroy it. Otherwise, he would have acted sooner in self-preservation. Instead, he returned to his same comfortable life. He went back to sleep.

In the dystopian novel *Brave New World*, author Aldous Huxley imagines a drug called soma inducing similar sleepiness, not to mention apathy, in the public. His book offers a more dramatic example (i.e., a pleasurable drug), but the mechanism is the same. It's defanging us. Demoralizing us.[9]

At this moment, most of our lives are still comfortable enough that we aren't doing enough (or anything at all) about the growing problem. Like Cheng, we are still waiting for someone else, like a city council member, to fix things. It's only when they don't that Cheng finally stands up.

Even then, we are left to wonder if it's too late.

It's not *at all* too late for us in real life. We exist at a unique and pregnant moment in time between the old order and the rise of the new. The future remains uncertain and undecided—a time meant for dreamers and heroes.

The nineteenth-century American essayist Ralph Waldo Emerson once said the following in gratitude for the tumultuous time he was also living through:

> If there is any period one would desire to be born in, is it not the age of revolution; when the old and the new stand side by side, and admit of being compared; when the energies of all men are searched by fear and by hope; when the historic glories of the old can be compensated by the rich possibilities of the new era? This time, like all times, is a very good one, if we but know what to do with it.[10]

What to do with it? That's the question we must ask ourselves. So far, we have introduced decentralized innovations to combat techno-tyranny. They will certainly help in the coming years. But more is needed. Let's discuss three more ways to turn things around—to make it a "very good time" indeed.

Appealing to Constitutional Law

In 2021, I (Robert), as CEO of Crown Sterling, a pioneer of personal data sovereignty technologies, established a "Data Bill of Rights." The first of its kind, the declaration states that all digital assets are to be the intangible property of the original producers (people like you and me) under existing laws and protections granted by the U.S. Constitution:

> We believe that digital assets are the intangible personal property of the original producer and therefore are protected by the United States Constitution, including the 4th and 5th Amendments; the United Nations Universal Declaration of Human Rights, including Articles 12 and 17; the Charter of Fundamental Rights of the European Union, including Articles 7 and 8; and the European Convention for the Protection of Human Rights and Fundamental Freedoms, including Article 8.[11]

Even this declaration isn't enough. In the coming years, it will be up to us to mount a legal strike against surveillance capitalists and the lawmakers who enable them to profit off people and control them using their data. Likewise, legal precedent must ensure that people's data remain their own intangible property, not would-be assets for plundering and exploitation. With data now globally recognized as the world's most valuable asset, the stakes have never been higher or more necessary.

Getting Politically Involved

In our story, Cheng starts out as the last person we would expect to mount a political run for city office. Shy and reserved, he can barely summon the will to speak up during public comments. It's only when life becomes so unbearable—and his rights get so trampled—that he throws his hat in the ring.

Good on our avatar—we applaud him for taking that bold step. Unfortunately, he's not real, and neither is his campaign. Instead, we need actual people to step up into public life as true public servants. Throughout this book, we have made the case that our struggle is not at all a Right-versus-Left issue. *It's a people issue.*

As we all know, social media has atomized us in recent years, superficially dividing individuals into tribes and echo chambers. Neither side wants to listen to the other; each points the finger at the other, casting them in the role of villain. This must change. If we ever hope to fix things, we must find commonality on both sides of the aisle.

Inspire Courage

It has been said that fear is contagious. COVID-19 showed us this in technicolor as people en masse stopped hugging or shaking hands and stayed six feet away from one another. Conversely, courage is also contagious. The bold words and actions of just one person can produce exponentially positive effects. That's because we live—for the first time ever—in a globally connected era.

This means that the next time you feel hopeless about the daunting challenges we face, think about Cheng appearing on TikTok. What do we mean by that? In our tale, Cheng stands in for another fictional character: Piglet. In Benjamin Hoff's 1992 book *The Te of Piglet*, the little porcine of *Winnie the Pooh* fame emerges as the unlikeliest of heroes.

Anyone who's familiar with the original series by A. A. Milne knows Piglet to be Pooh's best friend. Kind and loving, he's shy and cowardly, the last person—er, creature—to step into the fray.

Yet even as a "very small animal," Piglet manages to summon vast stores of courage and gumption to stand up for himself—and his friends. Like the time Owl's house blows down and bashful, diminutive

Piglet is the only one small enough—and bold enough—to squeeze out of the mailbox and get help.[12]

Right now, many of us similarly feel like very small animals up against a force with powers and resources we can scarcely imagine, much less confront. But the truth is, we are living in a story not unlike Piglet, Cheng, Demi, or any of the other characters we have met in the preceding chapters. And in this tale, we would like to reject the call to adventure that's been thrust on us. We would rather go back to our "ordinary world" of safety and security.

Unfortunately, that's not possible.

The only way out is through. Like any hero up against insurmountable odds, we must plunge forward—into the danger. The good news? You are not alone. *We* are not alone. And every action we take, every day, can be another tiny spark inspiring someone. Then the next person. And the next—until we emerge from this nightmare triumphant.

That can be our happy ending—if we just change the story we tell ourselves.

NOTES

FOREWORD

1. "The World's Most Valuable Resource Is No Longer Oil, but Data," *The Economist*, May 6, 2017, https://www.economist.com/leaders/2017/05/06/the-worlds-most-valuable-resource-is-no-longer-oil-but-data.

2. Shoshana Zuboff, *The Age of Surveillance Capitalism: The Fight for a Human Future at the New Frontier* of *Power* (New York: PublicAffairs, 2019).

3. Stephen Hawking, "Science AMA Series: Stephen Hawking AMA Answers!," *New Reddit Journal of Science*, October 8, 2015, https://www.reddit.com/r/science/comments/3nyn5i/comment/cvsdmkv/.

INTRODUCTION

1. Ralph Waldo Emerson, "The American Scholar," address delivered at Harvard College, Cambridge, MA, 1837, available at https://pressbooks.online.ucf.edu/johntest/chapter/ralph-waldo-emmerson/.

CHAPTER 1

1. "New Rule: Your Phone Is Turning You into an Asshole," *Real Time with Bill Maher Blog*, August 20, 2021, https://www.real-time-with-bill-maher-blog.com/index/2021/8/20/new-rule-your-phone-is-turning-you-into-an-asshole.

2. *The Matrix*, directed by Lana Wachowski and Lilly Wachowski (Burbank, CA: Warner Bros., 1999), DVD.

3. "Young People Are Sleeping with Their Phones; Their Parents Are Sleeping with People," *HuffPost*, September 16, 2013, https://www.huffpost.com/entry/sleep-phone-tablet-bed_n_3924161.

4. Jason Wise, "40 Smartphone Statistics 2022: How Many People Have Smartphones?," *EarthWeb*, August 1, 2022, https://earthweb.com/smartphone-statistics/.

5. Jory MacKay, "Screen Time Stats 2019: Here's How Much You Use Your Phone during the Workday," *RescueTime*, March 21, 2019, https://blog.rescuetime.com/screen-time-stats-2018/.

6. Josie Appleton, "Why We Must Oppose Vaccine Passports," *Sp!ked*, April 7, 2021, https://www.spiked-online.com/2021/04/07/why-we-must-oppose-vaccine-passports/.

CHAPTER 2

1. Joshua Hardwick, "Top 100 Most Visited Websites in the US," *Ahrefs*, January 1, 2021, https://web.archive.org/web/20210624030242/https://ahrefs.com/blog/most-visited-websites/.

2. John Action, letter to Bishop Mandell Creighton, April 5, 1887, in *Historical Essays and Studies* (London: Macmillan, 1907), paragraph 745.

3. George Orwell, *1984* (New York: Signet Classics, 1950).

4. Orwell, *1984*, 81.

5. Michael Fumento, "The Pandemic Is Political," *Forbes*, October 16, 2009, https://www.forbes.com/2009/10/16/swine-flu-world-health-organization-pandemic-opinions-contributors-michael-fumento.html?sh=d95a7d968992.

6. World Health Organization, "Q&A: Serology and COVID-19," June 9, 2020, https://web.archive.org/web/20200624152053/https://www.who.int/emergencies/diseases/novel-coronavirus-2019/question-and-answers-hub/q-a-detail/q-a-serology-and-covid-19.

7. World Health Organization, "WHO Director-General's Opening Remarks at the Media Briefing on COVID-19—12 October 2020," October 12, 2020, https://www.who.int/director-general/speeches/detail/who-director-general-s-opening-remarks-at-the-media-briefing-on-covid-19---12-october-2020.

8. World Health Organization, "WHO Director-General's Opening Remarks."

9. "Wikipedia: Verifiability," Wikipedia, August 26, 2022, https:// en.wikipedia.org/wiki/Wikipedia:Verifiability.

10. RT is the first Russian 24/7 English-language news channel that presents the Russian view on global news (see www.rt.com).

11. Chris Hedges, "Wikipedia—a Tool of the Ruling Elite," interview with Helen Buyniski, *On Contact*, October 21, 2018, https://www.rt.com/ shows/on-contact/441852-wikipedia-elite-journalist-discussion/.

12. Hedges, "Wikipedia."

13. Kevin Barrett, "Helen Buyniski: Wikipedia Is Rotten to the Core!," *Heresy Central*, November 30, 2018, https://kevinbarrett.heresycentral .is/2018/11/buyniski/.

14. Christopher Ketcham, "The Troubling Case of Chris Hedges," *New Republic*, June 11, 2014, https://newrepublic.com/article/118114/chris -hedges-pulitzer-winner-lefty-hero-plagiarist; "Chris Hedges," Wikipedia, June 12, 2014, https://web.archive.org/web/20140613063735/http:// en.wikipedia.org/wiki/Chris_Hedges.

15. Tom Huddleston Jr., "This 29-Year-Old Book Predicted the 'Metaverse'— and Some of Facebook's Plans Are Eerily Similar," CNBC *Make It*, November 3, 2021, https://www.cnbc.com/2021/11/03/how-the-1992 -sci-fi-novel-snow-crash-predicted-facebooks-metaverse.html.

16. Acton, letter to Bishop Mandell Creighton, paragraph 745.

CHAPTER 3

1. Tiffany Ap, "Victoria's Secret Has Hired Its First Male Model," *Quartz*, April 19, 2022, https://qz.com/2156655/victorias-secret-has-hired-its -first-male-model/.

2. Betsy Atkins, "Demystifying ESG: Its History and Current Status," *Forbes*, June 8, 2020, https://www.forbes.com/sites/betsyatkins/2020/06/08/ demystifying-esgits-history--current-status/?sh=674f84772cdd.

3. SustainFi, "30 ESG and Sustainable Investing Statistics," July 2, 2022, https://sustainfi.com/articles/investing/esg-statistics/.

4. Grace Chung, "The Asset Management Industry Has Surpassed $100 Trillion—and There's Still Room to Grow," *Institutional Investor*, July 8,

2021, https://www.institutionalinvestor.com/article/b1sls9m0wkdq9j/
The-Asset-Management-Industry-Has-Surpassed-100-Trillion-And-There
-s-Still-Room-to-Grow.

5. Heartland Institute, "Environmental, Social, and Governance (ESG)
Scores," accessed August 13, 2022, https://www.heartland.org/ESG/esg.

6. Elon Musk, Twitter post, April 2, 2022, 10:14 p.m., https://twitter.com/
elonmusk/status/1510485792296210434.

7. "I Support the Current Thing," *Know Your Meme*, 2022, https://
knowyourmeme.com/memes/i-support-the-current-thing?page=12377.

8. William Safire, "Useful Idiots of the West," *New York Times*, April 12, 1987,
http://therabbithole.wiki/useful-idiots-of-the-west-by-william-safire-new
-york-times-apr-1987/.

9. "Kim Iversen, "Elon Musk Blasts World Economic Forum's ESG Social
Score; Bill Gates Tops the List," *Rising*, April 6, 2022, https://www.youtube
.com/watch?v=-Cw27U1524A.

10. Iversen, "Elon Musk."

11. Iversen, "Elon Musk."

12. Ap, "Victoria's Secret Has Hired Its First Male Model."

13. Victoria's Secret, "Consciously Designing Positive Change: 2021 ESG
Report," 2021, p. 3, https://www.victoriassecretandco.com/static-files/
ebc70493-2a55-44f6-ad5b-a2ab02a6748d.

14. Victoria's Secret, "Consciously Designing Positive Change," 3.

CHAPTER 4

1. *Black Mirror*, season 3, episode 1, "Nosedive," directed by Joe Wright, aired
October 21, 2016, on Netflix.

2. Daniel J. Boorstin, *The Image: A Guide to Pseudo-events in America* (New
York: Vintage Books, 1992), 5–6.

3. Katie Canales, "China's 'Social Credit' System Ranks Citizens and Punishes
Them with Throttled Internet Speeds and Flight Bans If the Communist
Party Deems Them Untrustworthy," *Business Insider*, December 24, 2021,
https://www.businessinsider.com/china-social-credit-system-punishments
-and-rewards-explained-2018-4?op=1.

4.   Alexander Chipman Koty, "China's Corporate Social Credit System: What Businesses Need to Know," *China Briefing*, November 5, 2019, https://www.china-briefing.com/news/chinas-corporate-social-credit-system-how-it-works/.

5.   *Britannica*, s.v. "panopticon," accessed August 13, 2022, https://www.britannica.com/technology/panopticon.

6.   Carla Tardi, "Utilitarianism," *Investopedia*, June 10, 2022, https://www.investopedia.com/terms/u/utilitarianism.asp.

7.   U.S. Const. amend. VI.

CHAPTER 5

1.   Jack Kerouac, *On the Road* (New York: Penguin Books, 1999), 293.

2.   Kerouac, *On the Road*, 5.

3.   Benjamin Herold, "The Future of Big Data and Analytics in K-12 Education," *Education Week*, January 11, 2016, https://www.edweek.org/policy-politics/the-future-of-big-data-and-analytics-in-k-12-education/2016/01.

4.   "What Student Data Do Schools Collect?," August 25, 2014, https://iapp.org/news/a/what-student-data-do-schools-collect/.

5.   Iris Garner, "Data in Education, Part One of Two," Learning A–Z, accessed August 14, 2022, https://www.learninga-z.com/site/resources/breakroom-blog/data-in-education.

6.   Garner, "Data in Education."

7.   Shoshana Zuboff, *The Age of Surveillance Capitalism: The Fight for a Human Future at the New Frontier of Power* (New York: PublicAffairs Books, 2020).

8.   James Bridle, "The Age of Surveillance Capitalism by Shoshana Zuboff Review—We Are the Pawns," *The Guardian*, February 2, 2019, https://www.theguardian.com/books/2019/feb/02/age-of-surveillance-capitalism-shoshana-zuboff-review.

9.   Yuval Noah Harari, "Surveillance Is Getting under Our Skin—and That Should Alarm Us," *Al Jazeera*, May 31, 2020, https://www.aljazeera.com/opinions/2020/5/31/surveillance-is-getting-under-our-skin-and-that-should-alarm-us/.

10. Harari, "Surveillance Is Getting under Our Skin."

11. Harari, "Surveillance Is Getting under Our Skin."

CHAPTER 6

1. Rich Lowry, "Why Is Andrew Yang So Afraid of Automation?" *Politico Magazine*, October 16, 2019, https://www.politico.com/magazine/story/2019/10/16/andrew-yang-snake-oil-salesman-229855/.

2. Finn Murphy, "Truck Drivers Like Me Will Soon Be Replaced by Automation: You're Next," *The Guardian*, November 17, 2017, https://www.theguardian.com/commentisfree/2017/nov/17/truck-drivers-automation-tesla-elon-musk.

3. Justin Trudeau, Twitter post, March 31, 2020, 5:01 p.m., https://twitter.com/JustinTrudeau/status/1245139169934016517.

4. John Hayward, "Canada: Justin Trudeau Insists on Emergency Powers Despite No Active Protests," *Breitbart*, February 21, 2022, https://www.breitbart.com/national-security/2022/02/21/canada-justin-trudeau-insists-on-emergency-powers-despite-no-active-protests/.

5. Black Past, "(1857) Frederick Douglass, 'If There Is No Struggle, There Is No Progress,'" January 25, 2007, https://www.blackpast.org/african-american-history/1857-frederick-douglass-if-there-no-struggle-there-no-progress/.

6. Sheryl Sandberg, *Lean In: Women, Work, and the Will to Lead* (New York: Alfred A. Knopf, 2013), 157.

7. Henry David Thoreau, "Resistance to Civil Government," in *Becoming America: An Exploration of American Literature from Precolonial to Post-Revolution*, ed. Wendy Kurant (Dahlonega: University of North Georgia Press), 1177, https://web.ung.edu/media/university-press/becoming-america.pdf?t=1559065068636.

8. Martin Luther King Jr., *The Autobiography of Martin Luther King Jr.* (New York: Grand Central, 2001), 14.

9. "'I Have a Dream' Speech," History.com, accessed August 14, 2022, https://www.history.com/topics/civil-rights-movement/i-have-a-dream-speech.

10. Jose Nino, "Popular Anti-war Channel Geopolitics and Empire Gets Banned from Paypal," *Liberty Conservative News*, May 1, 2022, https://

libertyconservativenews.com/popular-anti-war-channel-geopolitics-and
-empire-gets-banned-from-paypal/.

11. Martin Luther King Jr., "Letter from a Birmingham Jail," April 16, 1963, University of Pennsylvania African Studies Center, accessed August 14, 2022, https://www.africa.upenn.edu/Articles_Gen/Letter_Birmingham.html.

CHAPTER 7

1. *Point Break*, directed by Kathryn Bigelow (Los Angeles, CA: Twentieth Century Fox, 1991), DVD.

2. Pamela Paresky, "Safetyism Isn't the Problem," *New York Times*, June 1, 2020, https://www.nytimes.com/2020/06/01/opinion/safetyism -coronavirus-reopening.html.

3. Nassim Nicholas Taleb, *Antifragile: Things That Gain from Disorder* (New York: Random House, 2014).

4. Matthew Lesh, "Is Safetyism Destroying a Generation?," *Quilette*, September 2, 2018, https://quillette.com/2018/09/02/is-safetyism -destroying-a-generation.

5. Peter Hancock, "Are Autonomous Cars Really Safer than Human Drivers?," *The Conversation*, February 2, 2018, https://theconversation.com/are -autonomous-cars-really-safer-than-human-drivers-90202.

6. Kai-Fu Lee and Chen Qiufan, *AI 2041: Ten Visions for Our Future* (New York: Currency, 2021), 29.

7. "Coronavirus: Peak District Drone Police Criticised for 'Lockdown Shaming,'" *BBC News*, March 27, 2020, https://www.bbc.com/news/uk -england-derbyshire-52055201.

8. Alicia Hope, "Privacy Concerns over Surveillance Drones Used in Monitoring Social Distancing," *CPO Magazine*, April 30, 2020, https:// www.cpomagazine.com/data-privacy/privacy-concerns-over-surveillance -drones-used-in-monitoring-social-distancing/.

9. Human Rights Watch, "Greece: New Biometrics Policing Program Undermines Rights," January 18, 2022, https://www.hrw.org/news/ 2022/01/18/greece-new-biometrics-policing-program-undermines-rights.

10. Human Rights Watch, "Greece."

CHAPTER 8

1. "Management Contract between Col. Tom Parker and Elvis Presley (1955)," PresLaw, accessed August 16, 2022, https://preslaw.info/management-contract-between-col-tom-parker-elvis-presley-1955.

2. "Chris Brown Slams Former Exploitative Manager Tina Davis Accusing Her of Sabotaging His Forthcoming CD with Leaks," *Judiciary Report*, February 25, 2014, https://judiciaryreport.com/chris_brown_slams_former_exploitative_manager.htm.

3. Helienne Lindvall, "Behind the Music: When Artists and Managers Fall Out," *The Guardian*, March 19, 2009, https://www.theguardian.com/music/musicblog/2009/mar/19/artist-manager-relationship.

4. Russell Brennan, "The Three Biggest Ways Musicians Get Ripped Off (and How to Avoid Them)," *Lateral Action*, accessed August 16, 2022, https://lateralaction.com/articles/music-business/.

5. Dejo Andersson, "How Record Labels Screw Artists," Eleven B Studios, accessed August 14, 2022, https://elevenbstudios.com/how-record-labels-screw-artists/.

6. "The Death Spiral of Napster Begins," History.com, November 16, 2009, https://www.history.com/this-day-in-history/the-death-spiral-of-napster-begins.

7. Tom Clayton, "15 Best Pandora Alternatives 2022," *Rigorous Themes*, May 19, 2021, https://rigorousthemes.com/blog/best-pandora-alternatives/.

8. Alexander Billet, "Spotify's Streaming Model Is Based on Exploitation," *Jacobin*, December 8, 2020, https://jacobin.com/2020/12/spotify-streaming-model-exploitation-class-conflict/.

9. "What Are NFTs and Why Are Some Worth Millions?" *BBC News*, September 23, 2021, https://www.bbc.com/news/technology-56371912.

10. Brandon Stoner, "NFTs for Musicians: A New Cash Source for Creatives?," *GearNews*, May 15, 2021, https://www.gearnews.com/nfts-for-musicians/.

CHAPTER 9

1. For the complete monologue, see George Carlin, "Life Is Worth Losing," November 5, 2005, Beacon Theater, New York City, https://www.youtube.com/watch?v=Nyvxt1svxso.

2. "Bash Presses Mayorkas about '1984' Comparisons to Disinformation Board," CNN, May 1, 2022, https://www.youtube.com/watch?v=tVty_rrKCO4.

3. "Summary: H.R.3359—115th Congress (2017–2018)," Congress.gov, November 16, 2018, https://www.congress.gov/bill/115th-congress/house-bill/3359.

4. European Commission, "Tackling Online Disinformation," accessed August 15, 2022, https://digital-strategy.ec.europa.eu/en/policies/online-disinformation.

5. European Commission, "Tackling Online Disinformation."

6. "Rand Paul Calls Out 'Disinformation Governance Board,'" *Capital Hill News*, accessed August 16, 2022, https://capitalhillnews.com/rand-paul-calls-out-disinformation-governance-board/.

7. Michael W. Chapman, "Sen. Paul to DHS' Mayorkas: 'The Greatest Propagator of Disinformation' Is the 'U.S. Government,'" *CNS News*, May 9, 2022, https://www.cnsnews.com/index.php/article/washington/michael-w-chapman/sen-paul-dhs-mayorkas-greatest-propagator-disinformation-us.

8. Taylor Lorenz, "How the Biden Administration Let Right-Wing Attacks Derail Its Disinformation Efforts," *Washington Post*, May 18, 2022, https://www.washingtonpost.com/technology/2022/05/18/disinformation-board-dhs-nina-jankowicz/.

9. Lorenz, "How the Biden Administration."

10. Carlin, "Life Is Worth Losing."

11. *Network*, directed by Sidney Lumet (Burbank, CA: Warner Bros. Entertainment, 1976), DVD.

12. Gab, "About Gab.com," accessed August 15, 2022, https://develop.gab.com/about.

13. See the IPFS website, at https://ipfs.tech.

14. See the *Washington Post* home page, at https://www.washingtonpost.com.

15. Paul Farhi, "*Washington Post* to Be Sold to Jeff Bezos, the Founder of Amazon," *Washington Post*, August 5, 2013, https://www.washingtonpost.com/national/washington-post-to-be-sold-to-jeff-bezos/2013/08/05/ca537c9e-fe0c-11e2-9711-3708310f6f4d_story.html.

16. "The World's Most Powerful People," *Forbes*, accessed August 15, 2022, https://www.forbes.com/powerful-people/list/#tab:overall.

17. Dylan Thomas, "Do Not Go Gentle into That Good Night," in *The Poems of Dylan Thomas* (New York: New Directions, 2003), 239.

CHAPTER 10

1. "Declaration of Independence: A Transcription," National Archives, June 8, 2022, https://www.archives.gov/founding-docs/declaration-transcript.

2. World Economic Forum, "Interview: Klaus Schwab," January 10, 2016, https://www.youtube.com/watch?v=XQWoMy-URPk.

3. *Wall Street Journal*, "Rahm Emanuel on the Opportunities of Crisis," November 19, 2008, https://www.youtube.com/watch?v=_mzcbXi1Tkk.

4. World Economic Forum, "The Great Reset," accessed August 16, 2022, https://www.weforum.org/great-reset.

5. Klaus Schwab, *COVID-19: The Great Reset* (Geneva, Switzerland: World Economic Forum, 2020), Kindle loc. 89, section 1.3.3, paragraph 2.

6. Schwab, *COVID-19*.

7. World Economic Forum, "8 Predictions for the World in 2030," November 18, 2016, https://www.youtube.com/watch?v=4zUjsEaKbkM.

8. Xander Landen, "Shanghai Residents Scream from Windows, Get Drone Lockdown Warning: Videos," *Newsweek*, April 10, 2022, https://www.newsweek.com/shanghai-residents-scream-windows-get-drone-lockdown-warning-videos-1696732; Alice Su, Twitter post, April 5, 2022, 1:21 p.m., https://twitter.com/aliceysu/status/1511558828802068481.

9. Aldous Huxley, *Brave New World* (New York: HarperCollins, 2017).

10. Ralph Waldo Emerson, "The American Scholar," address delivered at Harvard College, Cambridge, MA, 1837, available at https://pressbooks.online.ucf.edu/johntest/chapter/ralph-waldo-emmerson/.

11. Crown Sterling, "Crown Sterling Declares 'Data Bill of Rights' for Consumers," June 14, 2021, https://www.crownsterling.io/newsroom/data-bill-of-rights/.

12. A. A. Milne, *Piglet Does a Very Grand Thing* (London: Methuen, 1977).

ABOUT THE AUTHORS

ROBERT GRANT holds a BA from Brigham Young University and an MBA from Thunderbird School of Global Management. He was formerly CEO and president of Bausch and Lomb Surgical.

Robert is the founder, chairman, and managing partner of Strathspey Crown LLC, a growth equity holding company with a broad portfolio of company and asset holdings spanning healthcare, clean energy, social media, and financial technology. In addition, he is the founder, chairman, and CEO of Crown Sterling Limited LLC, provider of quantum-secure encryption and compression technologies based on novel discoveries in geometry and mathematics. He is also an accomplished artist and musician.

He is the coauthor (with Dr. Talal Ghannam) of *Philomath*, a unique book that unifies various scientific and artistic disciplines through numbers and geometry.

MICHAEL ASHLEY is a former Disney screenwriter and the author of more than thirty-five books on numerous subjects. He coauthored *Own the A.I. Revolution*, which launched at the United Nations and was named by Soundview as one of 2019's top business books.

A columnist for *Forbes* and *Becker's Hospital Review*, Michael serves as a member of City AI, an organization enabling the responsible development and application of artificial intelligence. An in-demand keynoter, he is also an official speaker for Vistage.

Michael taught screenwriting as a professor at Chapman University. His writing has been featured on KTLA and Fox Sports Radio and in *Entertainment Weekly*, *HuffPost*, *Newsbase*, *Fast Company*, the *National Examiner*, the United Nation's *ITU News Magazine*, the *Orange County Business Journal*, and the *Orange County Register*.